Sarah Tyson Heston Rorer

How to Cook Vegetables

Sarah Tyson Heston Rorer
How to Cook Vegetables
ISBN/EAN: 9783744783323

Printed in Europe, USA, Canada, Australia, Japan

Cover: Foto ©Andreas Hilbeck / pixelio.de

More available books at **www.hansebooks.com**

VEGETABLES.

BY

MRS. S. T. RORER,

PRINCIPAL OF THE PHILADELPHIA COOKING SCHOOL; EDITOR HOUSEHOLD
NEWS; AUTHOR OF MRS. RORER'S COOK BOOK, ETC., ETC.

SIXTH EDITION.

PUBLISHED BY

W. ATLEE BURPEE & CO.,
PHILADELPHIA.
1896.

COPYRIGHT, 1890,
BY W. ATLEE BURPEE & CO.,
PHILADELPHIA, PA.

PRESS OF WM. F. FELL & CO.,
1220-24 SANSOM STREET,
PHILADELPHIA.

PUBLISHER'S PREFACE.

The frequent receipt of inquiries as to the method of using certain Vegetables which are not generally grown in America suggested to us the advisability of having prepared a book on HOW TO COOK VEGETABLES. With this end in view we invited Mrs. S. T. Rorer to write the following pages.

Mrs. Rorer needs no introduction to the Housekeepers of America. As Principal of the Philadelphia Cooking School and Author of "Mrs. Rorer's Cook Book," she is known throughout the United States. In presenting another edition of a deservedly popular book we are pleased to announce that, "How to Cook Vegetables" has met with a success far beyond our most sanguine expectations. It is a book for every housewife and for every home.

In order to prevent needless correspondence from the book trade, we would state that "How to Cook Vegetables" is not published for sale, but for distribution among our customers as a premium, on the following conditions:—Any purchaser of Seeds, Bulbs, or Plants to the amount of $3.00 is entitled to receive, if a request accompanies the order, a copy bound in paper covers, while every purchaser to the amount of $5.00 is entitled to receive a copy substantially bound in cloth.

W. ATLEE BURPEE & CO.

Philadelphia, Feb. 15, 1895.

CONTENTS.

	PAGE
PREFACE,	vii
HOW TO COOK VEGETABLES,	9
PICKLING,	50–75
CREAM VEGETABLE SOUPS,	109
VEGETABLE SOUPS,	117
SALADS,	122
SALAD DRESSINGS,	124
CANNING,	138
SEASON FOR PICKLING,	150
BILLS OF FARE,	158

HOW TO COOK VEGETABLES.

Few things show the difference between comfortable and slovenly housekeeping more quickly than the dressing of vegetables. Potatoes, one of the most important of vegetables (served in nearly every household once a day), are rarely cooked in a wholesome or even palatable manner; out of every ten plates that come to the table but one will be found perfect. All green vegetables should be freshly gathered, washed in cold water, and cooked in freshly boiled water until tender, not a moment longer. After water has boiled for a time, it parts with its gases and becomes hard, and most vegetables are better cooked in soft water. It is a well-known fact that all vegetables containing casein, such as split peas, lentils, or beans, do not boil soft or tender in hard water. The salts of lime, sulphate, or gypsum which these seeds contain coagulate the casein, which renders the seeds unpalatable and unwholesome. The solvent power of pure soft water has such an effect upon these same vegetables when green that it will entirely destroy the firmness, color and outside covering (skin), allowing the juice to pass out into the water. Consequently, it must be remembered that all green vegetables must be cooked in hard water, and all dry vegetables in soft. A teaspoonful of common salt added to a gallon of water hardens it at once. A half teaspoonful of bicarbonate of soda to a gallon of water renders it soft.

Young, green vegetables should be cooked in boiling, salted water. Onions, if boiled in pure, soft water, are almost tasteless, and all the after-salting cannot restore to them the sweet saline taste and the strong aroma which they possess when boiled in salted water.

If green vegetables become wilted, sprinkle them with cold water. Do not soak them in salted water, as this toughens them. Peas, beans, and lentils are the most nutritious of all vegetable substances. They are said to contain as much carbon as wheat, and almost double the amount of nitrogen. The nitrogenous elements of these vegetables, consisting chiefly of vegetable casein, shows at once that we must arrange with care our daily bills of fare; and housekeepers are frequently at a loss to know just what kind of vegetables should be served with different kinds of meats, game, and fish to make them combine properly. A thorough acquaintance with these facts cannot be too highly estimated, as it is not a matter of fashion, but a necessity; for instance, if a man has baked beans for his dinner, he should certainly have served with them pork; the beans being nitrogenous, the meat must fill in the carbon. While we arrange our daily bills of fare in proper proportions to satisfy each organ, peace and harmony prevail in the system, but let us take too much liberty, and serve mashed potatoes daily with our pork and see what happens. An excitement is at once produced; each organ makes a strong effort to reject its enemy, and the whole system becomes out of order. Still, we fail to read this lesson of nature, teaching us to keep out of our stomachs all things that overload and crowd any such organ.

Why do we eat butter on our bread, or why should we serve potatoes with our lean beef, or (as I have said) pork with our beans? Simply to nourish ourselves properly. Bear in mind that during the process of living we use up and cast away certain matter which must be replaced by equivalent substances, and these substances must be found in some of our own elements. Albumen must be replaced by albumen, fibrine by fibrine, etc.

Dropping the scientific combination, there is a sense of taste that must also be consulted, to keep up the appetite. Certain vegetables seem particularly adapted to accompany certain meats. Fancy, for instance, a dish of corn passed with a fowl, or a dish of mashed turnips with boiled fish. The sight of such a combination would rob a sensitive person of appetite at once.

We serve, then (or should do so), potatoes with our roasted beef, rice with our mutton, beans and apple sauce with our pork, rice and peas with young chickens.

Cream vegetable soups should be accompanied with squares of toasted bread; oyster and clam soups with pickles and crackers. Croûtons go nicely with purées, boiled rice with gumbo; sliced cucumbers and potatoes should be served with fish. Where fish forms the main meat dish of a dinner, tomatoes and macaroni may also be served. Peas and tomatoes especially blend with ham and sweetbreads; mushrooms with chicken and sweetbreads. Corned beef is made more appetizing by a dish of carrots, stewed turnips, cabbage, string beans, kohl-rabi, and may also, be garnished with pickled beets. Roasted fowl may have as a garnish rice croquettes and baked tomatoes. Peas and macaroni may also accompany.

Roast turkey—with cranberry sauce or acid jelly, peas, tomatoes, or cauliflower. Spinach should be served with lamb or mutton. Apple sauce or fried apples, sweet or white potatoes, and tomatoes blend also with pork. With baked or boiled ham, fried turnips, sweet or white potatoes, broccoli or any of the cabbage family may be served. Fried potatoes join nicely with beefsteaks, tomato sauce with breaded chops and veal cutlets. Chicken croquettes are pretty and appetizing with green peas or served with lettuce or French dressing; lobster cutlets with lettuce, water-cress, corn-salad and sorrel with French dressing.

Broiled or baked blackbirds may be served with the salad course; also frogs' legs and fried shrimps. Calves' liver (baked) should have served with it squash, mashed potatoes or stuffed egg plant. Stewed cucumbers, corn, lima beans, peas, tomatoes may be served with almost every kind of meat. Bear in mind that corn must never accompany poultry or game. Boiled mutton (of course) must have caper sauce, boiled rice, cauliflower or stewed cabbage. Fried cabbage goes nicely with stewed beef.

Remember that while vegetables are plentiful, cheap and wholesome, they must never be served in too large quantities or in too great a number at one time. Cauliflower and asparagus, for instance, are better served as a course, alone; artichokes the same. Where fish is not easily obtained, a nicely cooked vegetable may be served as a second course, following the soup.

Turnips, carrots, parsnips and beets contain very little nourishment. For this reason they should always be served with concentrated food. They produce the necessary waste for proper intestinal action.

FRENCH ARTICHOKES.

French artichokes have a large, scaly head, like the cone of the pine tree.

Strip off the coarse, outer leaves, cut the stalks off about an inch from the bottom, wash well in cold water. Throw them in boiling water, add a teaspoonful of salt, and boil gently until the outer leaves are tender (about one and a half hours). Then take them from the fire, lift them carefully with a skimmer, place them upside down on a plate to drain. Arrange in a circle on a heated dish, tops up (of course), pour over them Béchamel or sauce Hollandaise, or English melted butter sauce, and serve.

BAKED ARTICHOKES.

Boil six artichokes for one and a half hours, drain as directed in preceding recipe. When thoroughly dry, tie a thin slice of pork around each artichoke, put a slice of onion on top and stand them in a baking dish. Chop fine two ounces of bacon, put it in the frying pan with two chopped shallots, six mushrooms, a tablespoonful of parsley, and a half pint of stock. Bring to boiling point and pour it into the centre of the artichokes, replacing the slice of onion. Put them in a moderate oven and bake for three-quarters of an hour. Then remove the slices of pork, dish the artichokes, fill the centres with sauce Hollandaise and serve.

FRIED ARTICHOKES.

Boil and drain six artichokes. Put them in a bowl, sprinkle them with vinegar, and dust with salt and pepper, and stand aside for one hour.

Break an egg into a soup dish, beat it lightly, add a tablespoonful of warm water. Dip the artichokes first into this and then into flour, and fry in smoking hot fat. Serve with sauce Tartare.

ARTICHOKES AS A BASIS FOR JARDINIÈRE
(of vegetables).

Remove the outer leaves of six artichokes, cut off the tops and also the furze which adheres to the bottom. Boil and drain them. While they are boiling prepare the Macédoine.

Cut two small carrots and one turnip, into shapes, with the vegetable cutter. Put them into a saucepan of salted water and boil until tender. In another saucepan boil a small quantity of string beans; in another a dozen asparagus tips or a few flowerets of cauliflower, and a half pint of green peas. When these are done, drain, and mix them carefully together. Make a half pint of Spanish sauce; mix them gently with it. When the artichokes are done, drain, and trim them perfectly round. Fill them with the Macédoine of vegetables and serve them as a garnish to beef à la mode, fillet of beef, braised turkey or braised leg of mutton.

ARTICHOKES, à l'ITALIENNE.

Trim and boil the artichokes as directed for sauce Hollandaise. After they are drained, remove all the outer leaves, using only the "choke." Arrange these in a circle, one slightly overlapping the other, and pour over them Italian sauce.

STUFFED ARTICHOKES.

12 artichokes,	½ pound of white meat of
2 tablespoonfuls of cream,	chicken,
1 tablespoonful of chopped parsley,	1 ounce of cooked ham,
	Grating of nutmeg,
Salt and pepper to taste.	

Boil and drain the artichokes; chop the chicken and ham fine, and add to it all the other ingredients. Fill the hollow part of the artichokes with this force-meat. Stand them in a buttered baking pan, and bake them in a quick oven fifteen minutes. Dish and pour around them plain Cream Sauce.

JERUSALEM ARTICHOKES.

This vegetable is derived from a plant belonging to the sunflower tribe, and is an entirely different production from the French artichoke. The root was cultivated in Europe before the common potato was introduced, but, unlike the potato, this tuber resists the action of the frost and is consequently allowed to remain in the ground during the winter, and is collected for use when required. On account of the absence of starch granules, it does not become mealy and dry, as the potato, and requires great care in cooking. Of course, a vegetable remaining in a sodden, watery condition is less digestible than a dry and mealy one.

The artichokes should be used while fresh, washed and scraped, and thrown into cold water immediately, to prevent discoloration. When ready to cook, throw them in boiling water, and add a teaspoonful of salt, and boil for forty minutes. Watch them closely, as they will become hard and tough if over-cooked. Drain, and serve them with Cream Sauce or sauce Hollandaise.

JERUSALEM ARTICHOKES (à la VINAIGRETTE).

Scrape the artichokes, throw them into cold water, and when ready to serve, cut them into thin slices, with a silver fork. Arrange them neatly on lettuce leaves and pour over them the following sauce :—

Put a salt-spoon of salt into a bowl, add a teaspoonful of water, stir until dissolved. Then add a tablespoonful of vinegar and work in gradually three tablespoonfuls of oil. If the oil floats and does not mingle with the vinegar, add another tablespoonful. Stir or rub constantly for about five minutes. Add a dash of cayenne and pour it over the artichokes. This, of course, should be served at once.

JERUSALEM ARTICHOKES (à la LYONNAISE).

Scrape the artichokes, throw them into cold water; cut them into slices, boil in salt water for twenty minutes. Drain and dry on a towel.

Put a tablespoonful of butter in a frying pan and add one onion, sliced; fry until slightly colored. Then add the artichokes; toss until they are a light brown. Dust with salt and pepper, dish, sprinkle over them chopped parsley and serve.

PICKLED JERUSALEM ARTICHOKES.

Boil the artichokes as directed for Jerusalem Artichokes, drain, and put them in a stone jar. To every quart of artichokes allow one pint of cider vinegar, one bay leaf, one slice of onion, four whole cloves and a blade of mace. Put the vinegar in a porcelain-lined kettle with all the other ingredients, stand it over a moderate fire and bring slowly to boiling point; then pour it over the artichokes and stand away to cool.

They will be ready to use in twenty-four hours, and will keep two weeks.

BOILED ASPARAGUS.

Wash the asparagus carefully in cold water, and peel the white ends; throw each stalk as soon as finished into cold water. When ready to cook, tie into small bundles and throw into a kettle of boiling water. Add a teaspoonful of salt; boil twenty minutes.

While the asparagus is boiling, toast squares of stale bread, cut off the crusts; butter the toast while hot and put it on a heated platter. When the asparagus is done, drain, cut the strings, and place it on the toast, heads all one way.

Put a tablespoonful of butter in a saucepan to melt, add to it one level tablespoonful of flour; mix until smooth, add a half pint of water in which the asparagus was boiled, stir continually until smooth and boil. Season it with a half teaspoonful of salt and a dash of pepper. Pour it over the asparagus, and serve.

STEWED ASPARAGUS.

Wash the asparagus in cold water, cut into pieces about one inch long, rejecting all the tougher parts. Put the pieces in a kettle, covering them with boiling water, add a teaspoonful of salt and boil thirty minutes; then drain in a colander. When thoroughly drained return to the kettle, dust the asparagus lightly with a tablespoonful of flour, add two ounces of butter and half a pint of cream or milk, half a teaspoonful of salt and a dash of pepper. As soon as this comes to boiling point it is ready to serve. Do not stir it or you will break the asparagus.

ASPARAGUS IN AMBUSH.

1 quart of asparagus tips,
1 pint of milk,
1 ounce of butter,
1 long, stale loaf of bread,
4 eggs (yolks),
Salt and pepper to taste.

Wash the asparagus tips, throw them into boiling water, add a teaspoonful of salt and boil fifteen minutes; then drain in a colander. Cut the bread into slices one and a half inches in thickness, remove the crusts; mark out the centre and remove the crumbs, leaving the slice in the form of a perfectly square box, the walls and bottom about one and a half inches thick. Brush the outside with melted butter and put into a quick oven until a golden brown. Fill the asparagus tips into the centres; arrange them on a neatly folded napkin. Stand them in a warm place while you make the sauce.

Put the milk on to heat in a double boiler, beat the yolks of the eggs until light, then stir them into the hot milk; stir until they just begin to thicken. Take quickly from the fire, add the butter, salt and pepper; pour this carefully into the boxes and serve at once.

ASPARAGUS, à la HOLLANDAISE.

1 bundle of asparagus,	2 ounces of butter,
2 tablespoonfuls of flour,	Yolks of two eggs,
1 tablespoonful of lemon juice,	1 teaspoonful of onion juice,
1 bay leaf,	1 tablespoonful of chopped parsley.

Wash, trim and boil the asparagus as directed for boiled asparagus. When done, drain and arrange neatly in a flat vegetable dish. Put the butter in a saucepan; when melted, add the flour; mix until smooth. Add a half pint of the water in which the asparagus was boiled; stir continually until boiling; add the bay leaf, onion, salt and pepper to taste. Stand this over hot water for five minutes; strain, add the parsley chopped fine, and the well-beaten yolks of the eggs; take from the fire and add the lemon juice. Pour this over the asparagus and serve as a vegetable course, by itself.

ESCALLOPED ASPARAGUS.

1 bundle of asparagus,	6 eggs,
2 ounces of butter,	2 tablespoonfuls of flour,
1 pint of milk,	1 level teaspoonful of salt,
A dash of white pepper,	½ cup of bread-crumbs.

Trim and boil the asparagus in salted water for twenty minutes, drain; hard boil the eggs, remove the shells and chop them fine. Put a layer of the asparagus in the bottom of a baking dish, then a sprinkling of the hard boiled eggs, another layer of asparagus and a sprinkling of egg, and so continue until the dish is full; have the last layer asparagus. Put the butter in a saucepan, add the flour, mix; add the milk; stir continually until boiling. Add the salt and pepper. Pour this gently into the dish, waiting until it settles to the bottom; sprinkle the breadcrumbs over the top and, if you like, sprinkle over also a tablespoonful of grated cheese. Bake in a quick oven until the bread is golden brown (about fifteen minutes).

This dish may be served alone as a course, or in the middle of a dinner as an entrée.

ASPARAGUS PEAS.

Cut the tops from one bundle of asparagus, throw them into boiling, salted water and boil fifteen minutes; drain in a colander. Then put into a saucepan with a tablespoonful (one ounce) of butter, a teaspoonful of sugar, a half teaspoonful of salt, a dash of pepper, four tablespoonfuls of cream mixed with the yolk of one egg. Toss gently over the fire for a moment and serve quickly in a heated dish.

STRING BEANS.

¼ peck of beans,   1 tablespoonful of butter,
Salt and pepper to taste.

Cut the blossom end of the bean and pull it back to remove the string; then pare a thin strip from the other edge of the pod. In this way only are you sure that every string is removed. Cut the beans into pieces one inch long, throw in clear, cold water for thirty minutes. Drain, put in a saucepan of boiling water with a teaspoonful of salt and one of butter; boil gently one hour. Drain, put them in a vegetable dish, add the butter, salt and pepper.

The first butter is to soften the beans while boiling.

STRING BEANS WITH CREAM.

Prepare the beans as directed in the preceding recipe. Put them in a saucepan of boiling water, add two ounces of ham, and boil gently one hour. Drain, remove the ham, return the beans to the saucepan. Add an ounce of butter, a gill of cream and a palatable seasoning of salt and pepper.

BAKED BEANS.

1 quart of small, white soup beans,
1 pound of pickled pork,
1 tablespoonful of molasses,
½ teaspoonful of mustard.

Soak the beans over night in cold water. In the morning wash well in a colander, put them into a kettle of cold water, bring quickly to boiling point; drain, throw this water away and cover with freshly boiled water. Score the rind of the pork and put into the kettle of beans; *simmer* until you may blow the skin off the beans. To do this take three or four beans in your hand, blow hard on them; if the skin cracks they are done; remove and drain at once. Put them into the bean pot, almost bury the pork in the centre, allowing the scored part to remain above the beans. Add a teaspoonful of salt to one pint of the water in which the beans are boiled; then add to it the mustard and molasses and pour over the beans. Put the lid on the bean pot and bake in a moderate oven for from six to eight hours. Add water as that on the beans evaporates. If you wish the beans for Sunday morning's breakfast, it is best to bake in a moderate oven all night.

As many persons are without bean pots and use an ordinary iron baking pan for the operation, they must remember that the pan must be covered carefully and watched closely, or the beans will break and become a soft, sticky mass. Two hours is sufficient time to allow if you use a baking pan.

KIDNEY BEANS, à la MAÎTRE d'HOTEL.

Take one quart of freshly shelled kidney beans, cover with boiling water, add a teaspoonful of salt and boil gently until tender. This can be ascertained by pressing the bean between the thumb and forefinger; if it mashes easily drain at once. Put them back into the saucepan, add a tablespoonful of butter, one tablespoonful of lemon juice; chop a teaspoonful of parsley very fine, add to it one gill of the liquor in which the beans were boiled, mix with it one tablespoonful of flour, add to the beans. Stir very gently until boiled and serve.

KIDNEY BEANS WITH BROWN SAUCE.

1 quart of kidney beans,
1 teaspoonful of salt,
A slice of onion,
1 pound of soup meat,
2 tablespoonfuls of butter,
2 tablespoonfuls of flour.

Put the beans into a saucepan with the meat and cover with boiling water, boil gently thirty minutes, then add a teaspoonful of salt, and boil until tender. Put the butter into a frying pan, and when very brown add the flour, and brown again. Then add one pint of the water in which the beans were boiled, stirring continually until boiling and smooth, add the onion chopped fine, and a palatable seasoning of salt and pepper. Drain the beans, add them to the sauce, *simmer* ten minutes and serve.

WHITE BEAN SAUTÉS.

This is a very good way of warming over cold beans. Put two tablespoonfuls of butter into a frying pan, with a teaspoonful of chopped onion and a tablespoonful of chopped parsley. Put in the beans, shake over the fire until the beans are thoroughly heated; sprinkle with a teaspoonful of salt, a dash of pepper and the juice of half a lemon. Serve very hot.

RED BEANS.

1 pint of beans,	1 onion,
1 carrot,	1 teaspoonful of sugar,
¼ pound of bacon,	Salt and pepper to taste.

Soak the beans over night in cold water; in the morning, wash, drain, put into a kettle with the bacon, onion, carrot and sufficient cold water to cover; add an eighth of a teaspoonful of bicarbonate of soda, and boil gently until the beans are tender (about one hour). When done, drain, put them into a vegetable dish, add two ounces of butter, and salt and pepper; serve at once. The bacon may be cut in thin slices and used as a garnish.

BEAN POLENTA.

1 pint of small, white soup beans,	1 tablespoonful of butter,
1½ tablespoonfuls of molasses,	1 tablespoonful of vinegar,
½ teaspoonful of French mustard,	Salt and pepper to taste.

Wash the beans and soak them over night in lukewarm water. In the morning, drain off this water, cover with fresh, cold water, bring slowly to a boil, and boil slowly one hour; drain again, cover with one quart of fresh, boiling water, and boil slowly another hour. When done, press through a colander, return to the kettle, add the butter, molasses, mustard, salt, pepper and vinegar; stir and boil ten minutes. Serve in a vegetable tureen.

BEAN CROQUETTES.

1 pint of white soup beans,	1 tablespoonful of molasses,
1 tablespoonful of vinegar,	1 tablespoonful of butter,
Salt and cayenne to taste.	

Boil the beans as directed in preceding recipe. When done, drain and press the beans through a colander, then add the other ingredients, mix well and stand away to cool. When cold, form into small balls, dip first in egg and then in bread crumbs, and fry in smoking hot fat.

LIMA BEANS, à la POULETTE.

1 pint of young beans,	½ pint of milk,
1 tablespoonful of butter,	2 level tablespoonfuls of flour,
Yolks of two eggs,	½ teaspoonful of salt,
Dash of pepper,	½ teaspoonful of onion juice.

Cover the beans with boiling water, add a speck of bicarbonate of soda, and boil thirty minutes. Drain, put the butter in a saucepan; when melted add the flour, mix; add the milk, stir until boiling; add the salt, pepper and onion juice. Take from the fire, add the yolks of the eggs, beaten. Dish the beans, pour over the sauce and serve very hot.

LIMA BEANS.

Cover the beans with freshly boiled water, add a teaspoonful of salt, and boil thirty minutes; drain, season with pepper and salt, and add to them sufficient butter to make them palatable. Half a cup of scalded cream may also be added; a sprig of mint may be boiled with the beans but removed before serving.

LIMA BEANS, (DRIED).

Soak one pint of beans in water over night. In the morning drain off this water and cover with fresh water. Two hours before dinner time drain again, cover with boiling, *soft* water, and boil thirty minutes. Drain again, cover with fresh, boiling soft water; add one-eighth of a teaspoonful of bicarbonate of soda and boil until tender. Drain, season with salt and pepper, dredge over them a tablespoonful of flour; add a tablespoonful of butter, a half-pint of cream, let them boil up once and serve; or they may be served with butter, salt and pepper.

All shelled beans, butter, kidney, case-knife and the small French beans may be cooked in precisely the same manner. The main point to be remembered is that all *dry* beans must be cooked in *soft* water and all *green* beans in *hard* water.

BOILED BEETS.

Wash carefully, but do not cut or scrape. If the skin is broken before cooking, the juice will go out into the water and the beets lose both flavor and color while cooking. Young beets will cook nicely in one hour, old ones—Mrs. Henderson says—require forever; but four hours' cooking will, as a rule, make them tender. If, however, they are tough and wilted, as is frequently the case in mid-winter, they should be soaked over night in cold water; if still wilted, they will never become palatable or tender. Beets should be put on to cook in boiling water and should be taken from the water at the end of the time given, thrown into cold water just a moment and the skin should be rubbed off with a towel. Then cut into slices, dish, dust with salt and pepper, pour a small quantity of melted butter over them and they are ready to serve.

Beets that are left over should be put at once into cold vinegar and used as pickles or as a garnish for potato salad.

BEETS WITH CREAM SAUCE.

Select sweet, white beets, and boil as directed in the preceding recipe. When the beets are done, rub off the skin and cut them into dice. Put them in a heated vegetable dish and pour over Cream Sauce.

TO PICKLE BEETS.

1 dozen good sized beets,   2 quarts of vinegar,
¼ ounce of mace,   ¼ ounce of ginger,
2 tablespoonfuls of grated horse-radish.

Boil the beets; when done remove the skins and cut them into any shape you please. They are prettier cut and gimped in the shape of wheels. Put them into a jar. Put the vinegar into a porcelain-lined kettle, add the mace, ginger and a salt-spoon of pepper. Bring to boiling point, take from the fire, add the horse-radish and pour, while hot, over the beets. Stand in a cold place and they will be ready to use in twelve hours.

SWISS CHARD OR SILVER BEET AS GREENS.

These are leaflets or mid-ribs of the white beet. Take them while young and tender, wash, tie into bundles, boil and dress precisely the same as asparagus on toast. Serve with them, sauce Hollandaise or English drawn butter.

This makes one of the most delicate and delicious of dishes.

BROCCOLI.

Pick off the leaves and cut the stalks close to the bottom of the bunch; throw into cold water half an hour, then tie in a piece of cheese-cloth to prevent breaking; put into a kettle of salted, boiling water and boil twenty minutes. Take out carefully, loosen the cheese-cloth, place the broccoli head up in a hot dish. Pour around it a half pint of Cream Sauce and serve very hot.

BRUSSELS SPROUTS.

1 quart of sprouts,   1 tablespoonful of salt,
2 ounces of butter,   2 tablespoonfuls of flour,
A dash of pepper.

Wash the sprouts and take off the dead leaves, throw

them into boiling water, add the salt and boil with the saucepan uncovered twenty minutes. Then drain into a colander; turn them into a heated dish. Melt the butter, add the flour, mix; add a pint of water in which the sprouts were boiled, stir until boiling, add the pepper, one tablespoonful of lemon juice, pour over the sprouts and serve.

Sprouts may also be served boiled with plain melted butter, salt and pepper, or boiled with Cream Sauce.

BRUSSELS SPROUTS, SAUTÉS.

Pick, wash and boil one quart of Brussels Sprouts; drain carefully, put them in a saucepan with two tablespoonfuls of butter, toss over a quick fire for about eight minutes, then add one tablespoonful of tarragon vinegar, one tablespoonful of chopped parsley, and a palatable seasoning of salt and pepper; serve very hot.

Sprouts may also be used, plain boiled, as a garnish for braised meats.

BORECOLE OR KALE.

Wash half a peck of kale thoroughly in cold water, changing the water as it becomes clouded, then pick over carefully, cut off the roots, wash again, drain by picking up in handfuls and shaking. Put this into a kettle with one pint of boiling water, stand over the fire and cook for thirty minutes; do not cover the kettle. Then drain in a colander, turn into a chopping tray and chop fine; it cannot be too fine. Put into a small saucepan, add two tablespoonfuls of cream, one tablespoonful of butter and a palatable seasoning of salt and pepper, stir over the fire until very hot. Serve on a heated dish, garnished with squares of buttered toast.

KALE WITH PORK.

Put a piece of salt pork into a kettle of cold water, allowing it to boil fifteen minutes to a pound. Three-quarters of an hour before it is done, have ready, washed and picked, the necessary quantity of kale, put it on with the pork, do not cover the kettle, and boil thirty minutes. When done, drain, put the pork in the centre of the dish and the kale around it; garnish with hard-boiled eggs. French dressing may also be poured around it.

BOILED CABBAGE.

Select a heavy, white head of cabbage, remove the outside leaves, cut into quarters and, if the head is large, again into eighths. Soak in cold water one hour, drain, cover with boiling water, let stand fifteen minutes or until cool. Press out this water gently and put the cabbage in a kettle nearly filled with boiling water; the cabbage *must* be covered or the odor will penetrate the entire house. Add a teaspoonful of salt and a small piece of Chili pepper; cover, and boil three-quarters of an hour. If the cabbage is old, it may perhaps require one hour's boiling. The first scalding and the Chili pepper are supposed to diminish the unpleasant odor usually thrown off; this we know—if the directions are carefully followed, cabbage may be cooked until thoroughly done, without the slightest odor in the house. When the cabbage is done, drain and serve with Drawn Butter or Cream Sauce.

CABBAGE WITH CORNED BEEF.

Wash the meat in cold water, put it into a large kettle and cover with cold water; *simmer* gently two hours or fifteen minutes to a pound. In the meantime, remove the outside leaves from a hard head of cabbage, cut into quarters and soak in cold water one hour, then add to the meat; *simmer* one hour. When done, put the meat in the centre of a large dish and arrange the cabbage neatly around it. Serve with tomato catsup, mustard or horse-radish sauce.

STEWED CABBAGE.

Cut a small head of cabbage into quarters and soak in cold water one hour, drain and shake; remove the hard part and chop the remainder rather fine. Put in a stewing pan with sufficient boiling water to cover it, add a teaspoonful of salt, boil twenty minutes. Drain in a colander, turn into a heated dish and pour over it, Cream Sauce.

STUFFED CABBAGE.

For this dish select a head of Savoy cabbage; the ordinary hard head cannot be stuffed. Put the whole head into a bowl and pour boiling water over it. Let it stand fifteen minutes, drain, cover again with boiling water, let it stand thirty minutes. While this is standing make the stuffing as follows:—

Wash two heaping tablespoonfuls of rice in cold water, boil twenty minutes; then mix it with a half pound of sausage meat, one tablespoonful of onion juice, one tablespoonful of chopped parsley and a dash of pepper. Mix all well together, drain, and gently press the water from the cabbage, then open it carefully to the very centre. Put in about a half teaspoonful of this mixture, fold over two or three of the little leaves, cover these leaves with a layer of the mixture. Fold over this the next layer of leaves, and so continue until each layer is stuffed. When finished, press all firmly but gently together. Tie the head in a piece of cheese-cloth, put in a kettle of salted, boiling water and boil two hours. When done, carefully remove the cloth, stand the cabbage in a deep, round dish, pour over it Cream Sauce and serve very hot.

SCALLOPED CABBAGE.

½ head of cabbage,
2 level tablespoonfuls of flour,
4 eggs,
2 ounces of butter,
1 pint of milk,
1 teaspoonful of salt,
Dash of pepper.

Wash and chop coarsely the cabbage, throw into a kettle of boiling, salted water and boil twenty minutes, drain in a colander. Have ready four hard-boiled eggs chopped fine. Put two tablespoonfuls or two ounces of butter in a saucepan; when melted, add two level tablespoonfuls of flour, add one pint of milk, stir continually until it boils; add the chopped eggs, one teaspoonful of salt and a dash of pepper. Put the cabbage in a baking dish, pour over the sauce, sprinkle with bread crumbs and bake in a quick oven fifteen minutes.

CABBAGE WITH PARMESAN CHEESE.

Remove the outer leaves and cut one head of Savoy cabbage in halves; throw into boiling, salted water and boil twenty minutes. Drain and put carefully in a baking dish, pour over a half pint of cream sauce, dust thickly with grated Parmesan or other cheese, then with bread crumbs; bake in a quick oven fifteen minutes.

CHARLESTON CABBAGE.

1 head of cabbage,
2 tablespoonfuls of sugar,
½ pint of cream,
4 tablespoonfuls of vinegar,
2 tablespoonfuls of olive oil,
1 egg,
Salt and pepper to taste.

Select a hard head of cabbage, cut it into halves, then

into eighths; put into a kettle of boiling, salted water, boil twenty minutes, drain. While it is boiling beat the egg until well mixed, add to it the cream. Put the vinegar, sugar, salt, pepper and oil into the saucepan, bring to boiling point, add the egg and cream, mix thoroughly, add the cabbage, cook one moment and serve very hot.

FRIED CABBAGE.

½ head of cabbage,
2 tablespoonfuls of vinegar,
2 ounces of butter.
A palatable seasoning of salt and pepper,

Wash and chop the cabbage rather fine, put into a kettle of salted, boiling water; boil twenty minutes and drain. Return to the kettle, add butter, vinegar, salt and pepper; stir until very hot and serve.

RED CABBAGE, à la FLAMANDE.

Take off the outer leaves of a hard head of red cabbage, cut it in pieces, cover with boiling water, let stand fifteen minutes; drain and chop fine. Put this into a porcelain-lined stewing pan with a tablespoonful of butter, one sliced onion, one bay leaf, two cloves, one teaspoonful of salt and a dash of pepper. *Simmer* slowly three-quarters of an hour, stirring occasionally. Take out the bay leaf, add one tablespoonful of fresh butter and serve at once.

Do not add water, as the cabbage will be sufficiently moist to prevent scorching.

RED CABBAGE, GERMAN STYLE.

Trim the leaves from two small, solid heads of red cabbage, divide them in halves; place the flat side downward on the table and cut the cabbage into slices a half inch thick. Put two tablespoonfuls or two ounces of butter in a large frying pan; when hot put in the slices of cabbage, add one teaspoonful of salt, three tablespoonfuls of vinegar, and one chopped onion. Cover the pan and place over a moderate fire to cook gently one hour. Serve very hot.

If care is taken in the preparation of this dish, it will be delicious.

PICKLED CABBAGE.

Chop sufficient cabbage to make one gallon, add one good-sized onion chopped, two red and two green peppers cut in small strips. (The onion may be omitted if not liked.) Put one layer of this in the bottom of a stone jar, sprinkle over one teaspoonful of salt, then one of cabbage, one of salt, and so continue until the cabbage is used. Cover and stand away over night. Next day drain thoroughly in a colander, pressing lightly; then put a layer of the cabbage in the bottom of a jar, sprinkle over a few mustard seeds, one or two whole cloves, then a layer of cabbage, dust with pepper; again a layer of mustard seed and one or two cloves, and so continue until the jar is nearly full. Do not pack tightly. Cover with good cider vinegar, waiting until it sinks to the bottom of the jar; then cover again until the cabbage is thoroughly moistened with vinegar. It is ready for immediate use and will keep seven or eight days.

PICKLED RED CABBAGE.

Cut hard heads of red cabbage into fine strips, place at once in a stone jar. Add to each layer, a half teaspoonful of salt and about six whole allspice and pepper-corns. Cover with cold vinegar and it is ready for immediate use.

SAUERKRAUT.

Shred the cabbage fine. Line the bottom and sides of a small keg with the green cabbage leaves, put in a layer of the cabbage about three inches thick, cover with four ounces of salt and pound down well, then another layer of cabbage and salt, and so on until the keg is full. Put a board on top of the cabbage and on this a heavy weight, and stand in a moderately warm place to ferment. The cabbage sinks when the fermentation begins and the liquor rises to the surface over the cover. Skim off the scum and stand the keg in a cool, dry cellar and it is ready to use. Cover it closely each time any is taken out. When you use it, wash it in warm water, and boil it with corned beef or salt pork the same as cabbage.

COLD SLAW.

1 quart of cut cabbage,
½ cup of cream (sour is best),
2 tablespoonfuls of vinegar,
2 eggs,
1 teaspoonful of salt,
A little pepper,
Butter the size of a walnut.

Cut the cabbage very fine and put it in an earthen bowl. Put the vinegar on to boil. Beat the eggs until light, add to them the cream and butter. Now add to these the boiling vinegar. Stir over the fire until boiling hot, add the salt and pepper, and pour over the cabbage, and it is ready to serve when very cold.

KOHL-RABI.

Kohl-rabi or kale-turnip, as it is sometimes called, is a cultivated variety of kale or cabbage, distinguished by the swelling of the stem, just above the ground, in a turnip form, to the size of a man's fist; the larger leaf-stalks springing from the swollen part. This swollen part is used for food. It may be served according to any of the recipes given for turnips; or, uncooked in slices—the same as radishes.

PICKLED PARSLEY.

Select perfect, curly heads of parsley, wash thoroughly in salt water, drain and shake till dry. Put into jars of cold vinegar and to each quart allow two tablespoonfuls of chopped horse radish. Cover and stand away for use.

This is especially nice in winter when it is impossible to get the fresh parsley, and may be used to garnish cold meat dishes, deviled eggs, tomatoes or hot spiced meats. Fresh green parsley may be used as a flavoring for sauces, soups, and all kinds of braised meats, and is the prettiest of all the garnishes.

PICKLED CARROTS.

Scrape and wash in cold water six good-sized carrots, cut in slices cross-wise; throw them into a kettle of boiling water, boil until tender, about three-quarters of an hour. Drain, put in a jar and pour over them cold vinegar, add one slice of onion, two bay leaves and a teaspoonful of celery seed. They will be ready to use in twelve hours.

These pickled carrots make a delightful garnish for cold meat dishes, potato salad, or may be served following soup with celery, olives, etc.

STEWED CARROTS, No. 1.

Scrape and cut into cubes sufficient carrots to make one pint. throw into a kettle of boiling water; cook three-quarters of an hour, then drain. Put two tablespoonfuls of butter in a saucepan, add a half pint of good stock and one tablespoonful of sugar. Boil rapidly ten minutes, take from the fire, add the beaten yolks of two eggs, a half teaspoonful of salt and a dash of pepper. Drain and dish the carrots, pour the sauce over them while very hot.

STEWED CARROTS, No. 2.

3 good-sized carrots,
1 tablespoonful of butter,
½ pint of milk,

1 teaspoonful of salt,
1 tablespoonful of flour,
Salt and pepper to taste.

Pare and quarter the carrots. Put them in a saucepan and cover with boiling water; add the salt and let them boil one hour and a half. When done, drain, place them on a hot dish and stand over boiling water to keep warm. Put the butter in a frying pan, let it melt; add the flour and mix. Do not brown. Now add the milk, salt and pepper. Stir until it boils and is smooth. Pour over the carrots and serve.

CARROT MARMALADE.

Wash and boil until tender four pounds of young carrots, drain and peel, then press them through a colander, put them into a porcelain-lined kettle with two pounds of sugar and a pint of water, add a few pieces of chipped lemon peel, the grated yellow rind of two oranges, a small piece of ginger root cut into pieces and two bay leaves; *simmer* gently until the proper consistency and put away in tumblers.

CAULIFLOWER WITH CREAM SAUCE.

Pick off the outer leaves, cut off the stem close to the bottom of the flowerets; wash the head well in cold water, then soak, the top downward, in a pan of clear, cold water one hour. Place the head in a vegetable basket or tie in a piece of cheese-cloth, stand in a kettle of boiling, salt water, stems downward; cover the kettle and boil gently thirty minutes, or until the cauliflower is tender. When done, lift carefully from the water; if in a basket, simply turn it out. If in a cloth, remove the cloth and stand the cauliflower in a round, shallow dish, stems downward. If two heads are cooked, place them in a platter, stems to the centre of the platter. Pour over Cream Sauce and serve.

Cauliflower cooked this way may be served as a separate course by itself.

STEWED CAULIFLOWER.

1 head of cauliflower,	4 slices of bread,
1 tablespoonful of butter,	6 mushrooms,
Yolks of three eggs,	½ teaspoonful of onion juice,
¼ teaspoonful of pepper,	1 tablespoonful of flour,
½ pint of stock,	Grating of nutmeg,

½ teaspoonful of salt.

For this select a cauliflower close and white. Pick off the outer leaves and break apart the flowerets; wash well in cold water, throw in a kettle of boiling water, add one teaspoonful of salt and boil briskly until the stalks feel tender (about twenty or twenty-five minutes). When done, lift carefully with a skimmer, place them on the squares of bread that have been toasted and buttered while hot. Put the butter in a saucepan, add the flour, mix; add the stock, stir continually until it boils; add the mushrooms chopped fine, cook a moment longer. Take from the fire, add the beaten yolks of the eggs, salt, pepper, nutmeg and onion juice. Pour this around the cauliflower and serve at once.

The sauce *must not* be boiled after the eggs are added or it will curdle.

CAULIFLOWER au GRATIN.

1 cauliflower,	1 tablespoonful of butter,
1 tablespoonful of flour,	½ pint of milk,
½ teaspoonful of salt,	4 tablespoonfuls of grated cheese.

Boil the cauliflower as directed in Cauliflower with Cream Sauce. When done, drain carefully and put into a baking dish. Put the butter in a frying pan, when melted add the flour, mix till smooth, add the milk, stir continually until it boils, then add the salt and cheese. Pour this over the cauliflower and serve at once.

BAKED CAULIFLOWER.

1 cauliflower,	1 tablespoonful of butter,
1 tablespoonful of flour,	½ teaspoonful of salt,
½ cup of bread crumbs,	1 bay leaf,
1 tablespoonful of chopped parsley,	½ pint of milk.

Wash the cauliflower, cut off the outer leaves and break the head into flowerets; throw into a kettle of boiling, salted water and boil thirty minutes. Drain, place in a baking dish.

Put the butter in a saucepan, add the flour, mix; add the milk, stir continually until it boils, add the bay leaf, parsley, salt and pepper. Stand this over boiling water ten minutes. Remove the bay leaf, pour the sauce over the cauliflower, sprinkle over the bread crumbs. Put here and there bits of butter, bake in a quick oven until the bread is a golden brown (about fifteen minutes).

PICKLED CAULIFLOWER.

¼ pound of English mustard,	½ ounce of turmeric,
2 tablespoonfuls of mustard seed,	½ gallon of vinegar,
1 cup of sugar,	1 gill of salad oil,
3 good-sized heads of cauliflower.	

Boil the cauliflower until tender, and divide it into flowereis. Put the vinegar in a porcelain-lined kettle; mix the mustard and turmeric together, moisten with a little cold vinegar, stir into the hot vinegar and continue until it begins to thicken. Add the sugar, mustard seed and oil, and stir again. Pour this while hot over the cauliflower. When cool, put away in glass or stone jars, and it is ready to use.

FRIED CELERY.

Remove the green leaves from the celery and cut the stalks into pieces five inches long. Cleanse thoroughly, cover with boiling water, stand aside fifteen minutes; drain and dry on a towel. Beat one egg without separating until the white and yolk are thoroughly mixed, add one tablespoonful of warm water. Take one cup of dry bread crumbs, add a half teaspoonful of salt and a dash of pepper. Dip the celery first in the egg and then in the crumbs; fry until crisp, in smoking hot fat. Drain and serve hot.

This is a very nice accompaniment to poultry and game.

CELERY WITH TOMATO SAUCE.

Trim the green ends from six roots of celery; do not separate the stalks, but cleanse the celery by plunging it in and out of cold water. Trim the roots and see that the celery is perfectly free from sand. Throw the bunches in a kettle of boiling water; add one teaspoonful of salt and boil twenty minutes. Drain, arrange on a flat dish, roots all one way, pour over one pint of tomato sauce and serve.

CELERY, à la FRANCAISE.

Wash and cut two roots of celery into pieces a half inch long, throw into a kettle of boiling water; add a teaspoonful of salt and boil twenty minutes. Drain in a colander. Put one tablespoonful of butter in a saucepan and add a level tablespoonful of flour, mix until smooth; add a pint of chicken stock, stir continually until it boils, add a half teaspoonful of salt, a dash of pepper, a half teaspoonful of onion juice and the celery. Cover and *simmer* gently ten minutes. Serve very hot.

CELERIAC OR TURNIP-ROOTED CELERY.

Pare one dozen of the celeriac, throw into cold water for thirty minutes. Then put in a saucepan, cover with boiling water, add a half teaspoonful of salt and boil thirty or thirty-five minutes. They should be tender when pierced with a fork. When done, drain, cut in slices, dish, cover with Cream Sauce and serve.

These roots also make a delightful salad dressed with Mayonnaise.

STEWED CELERY.

The green stalks that are not attractive on the table may be used in this way:—

Scrape and wash them clean. Cut in pieces one inch long, and soak in cold water for fifteen minutes; then put them into a saucepan of boiling water, add a teaspoonful of salt, and boil thirty minutes, or until tender. When done, drain in a colander and throw into cold water while you make the sauce. Put one tablespoonful of butter in a frying-pan; and, when melted, add one tablespoonful of flour; mix until smooth; add a half-pint of milk and stir *continually* until it boils; then add three tablespoonfuls of the water in which the celery was boiled, salt and white pepper to taste. Add the celery to this sauce, stir until thoroughly heated through, and it is ready to serve.

CELERY au JUS.

Scrape and wash the celery. Cut it in pieces one inch long; then put in a saucepan, cover with boiling stock, add a teaspoonful of salt and boil thirty minutes. Put one tablespoonful of butter in a frying-pan and stir until a dark brown; add to it one tablespoonful of flour, mix until smooth. Drain the celery, then add a half-pint of the liquor in which it was boiled to the butter and flour; stir *continually* until it boils, then add salt and pepper to taste. Put the celery in a heated dish, pour the sauce over it, and serve.

CHICORY WITH CREAM.

Wash a quarter of a peck of chicory, throw in a large kettle of salted water and boil half an hour. Then drain and throw into a pan of cold water five minutes. Drain and press gently until dry. Chop fine, put into a saucepan with two ounces of butter, a teaspoonful of sugar, a teaspoonful of salt and a grating of nutmeg; then sprinkle over an even tablespoonful of flour. Mix all this well together, add a gill of thick cream, stirring over the fire until boiling hot. Take from the fire. Beat the yolks of three eggs until light, add two tablespoonfuls of cream, stir this into the chicory. Turn into a heated dish and serve garnished with hard-boiled eggs.

CORN BOILED ON THE COB.

Corn should be cooked as quickly as possible after picking, as it heats and loses its sweetness. If necessary to keep over night, spread it out singly on the cold cellar floor; do this as quickly as you receive it. Do not open or tear the husks until ready to boil it. Then remove the husks and every thread of silk. Have ready a kettle of boiling water, throw in the corn and boil, after it begins to boil, five minutes. Long boiling destroys both the color and flavor of the corn and renders it indigestible. When done, take out carefully with a skimmer, place on a corn-cloth or napkin, throw the corners over to prevent the steam escaping; serve immediately.

While perhaps it is rather unusual to give recipes "how to eat," it is certainly an art to know just how to eat corn. Score every row of grains with a sharp knife, spread lightly with butter, dust with salt, and with the teeth press out the centre of the grains, leaving every hull fast to the cob. Corn thus eaten will not cause trouble or produce indigestion, as the hull is the only indigestible part. Small wooden skewers with quills of paper may be stuck in the ends of the cob and used as holders.

CORN BOILED IN THE HUSKS.

Remove the outer husks, leaving the cob covered with a layer of the young, light husks. These must be opened, of course, to enable you to take away the silk. Have ready a kettle of boiling water, throw in the corn and boil, after it begins to boil, ten minutes. When done, drain, serve in a napkin or corn-cloth as before. Do not remove the husks. Many persons think this the better way of boiling corn, as the husks prevent the sweetness from being drawn out into the water.

CORN FRITTERS.

1 dozen ears of corn,
½ pint of milk,
½ teaspoonful of salt,
2 eggs,
½ pound of flour,
1 teaspoonful of baking powder,
2 dashes of pepper.

Score the corn down the centre of each row of grains, then with a blunt knife press out the pulp, leaving the hull on the cob. Never grate corn, as in that way you get all the hull mixed with the pulp. To this pulp add the milk, salt, pepper, yolks of the eggs and the flour. Beat well. Beat the whites of the eggs to a stiff froth, add them to the baking powder, stir carefully until thoroughly mixed. Have ready a pan of deep lard, drop the mixture by spoonfuls into the boiling fat; brown on one side, then turn and brown on the other. Remove each one with a skimmer, drain on brown paper. Serve very hot.

Do not pierce the fritters with a fork, as it allows the steam to escape and makes the fritters heavy, Canned corn may be used, allowing one pint finely chopped.

STEWED CORN WITH TOMATOES.

Scald and peel six good-sized tomatoes, cut them in pieces, put them in a porcelain-lined kettle with a tablespoonful of butter and a slice of onion; stew slowly thirty minutes. Husk one dozen ears of corn, score down the centre of each row of grains, press out the pulp; add it to the tomatoes, cook ten minutes. Add another tablespoonful of butter and a palatable seasoning of salt and pepper. After adding the corn, watch carefully or the corn will settle to the bottom of the pan and scorch. Serve very hot.

SCALLOPED CORN.

Husk one dozen ears of corn, score and press out the pulp as previously directed. Scald, pare and cut fine six good-sized ripe tomatoes. Measure a half pint of stale bread crumbs. Put a layer of corn in the bottom of a baking dish, then a layer of tomatoes, then a sprinkling of bread crumbs, dust with salt and pepper; another layer of corn, then the tomatoes, bread crumbs, and so continue until all the ingredients are used, having the last layer bread crumbs. Put bits of butter over the top and bake in a moderate oven a half hour.

STEWED CORN.

Husk the corn, remove the silk; throw the ears into boiling water, boil five minutes; drain and cool; draw a sharp knife down the centre of each row of grains, press the corn out with a blunt knife, put in a saucepan, and to each pint add one teaspoonful of sugar, a half teaspoonful of salt, one dash of pepper, a half cup of cream. Cook. carefully for five minutes and serve very hot.

The latter part of the preparation is best done in a double boiler, as corn scorches very quickly.

TO WARM OVER COLD CORN.

Cold corn left from dinner may be cut carefully from the cob, covered with milk, put in a double boiler and cooked ten minutes. Add butter, salt and pepper to taste.

CORN GRIDDLE CAKES.

1 quart of scraped corn,
½ pint of milk,
4 eggs,
½ pint of flour,
1 tablespoonful of melted butter,
½ teaspoonful of salt.

Scrape the corn and press out as previously directed on Page 40, Corn Fritters; add the yolks of the eggs, milk, salt, melted butter and flour. Beat well, then stir in carefully the stiffly beaten whites of the eggs and bake at once on a hot griddle. Do not add baking powder or extra flour, if you can possibly handle them.

CORN GEMS.

1 pint of corn,
1 pint of milk,
1 tablespconful of butter,
3 eggs,
1½ pints of flour,
½ teaspoonful of salt,
2 teaspoonfuls of baking powder.

Scrape the corn and press it out as directed, on Page 40, Corn Fritters. Add to it the milk, salt, yolks of the eggs and flour. Beat well and stir in carefully the whites of the eggs beaten to a stiff froth and the baking powder. Bake in greased gem pans in a moderate oven thirty minutes; serve hot. These, if carefully made, are delicious breakfast cakes.

TO HULL CORN.

Put one pint of clear, hard wood ashes in two quarts of cold, soft water; boil fifteen minutes, stand aside until the water is perfectly clear, then drain it off carefully. Dip your finger in the water, rub it against your thumb, and if it feels slippery, add as much cold water as will cover two quarts of white corn. Return the corn and the lye to the porcelain kettle, boil gently until the hulls begin to start; then with a skimmer dip out the corn and throw it into a pan of clear, cold water. When you have it all out rub thoroughly with the hands to remove the hulls and also to cleanse the corn of the lye. It may be necessary to rub it through three or four fresh waters, but this washing must continue until the corn is perfectly free from the taste of lye. Then put it into clear water and boil until tender, about three or four hours. Drain, add a quarter of a pound of butter and a palatable seasoning of salt and pepper. A half pint of cream may also be added, if liked. This corn having been soaked in an alkali to remove the hull, has, of course, lost a quantity of corn oil and therefore makes a good summer food.

TO DRY CORN.

Remove the husks, score down the centre of each row of grains, then press out the pulp, leaving every particle of hull fast to the cob. Spread this pulp on tin sheets or in ordinary baking pans; dry in the hot sun or in a very moderate oven, watching carefully and stirring occasionally that the corn may not lose its color. If the oven is just right three hours should dry it. As soon as it is thoroughly dry take from the oven, and when cold put it into bags and hang in a cool, dry place.

TO COOK DRY CORN.

Cover one pint of corn with warm water and soak over night. In the morning, if the corn has absorbed all the water, add more and cook slowly on the back part of the stove for two hours. At the end of this time the water should be entirely absorbed; if not, remove the lid and boil rapidly a few moments, then add a half cup of cream, one tablespoonful of butter, a palatable seasoning of salt and pepper. Serve very hot.

CORN-SALAD.

Corn-salad may be washed thoroughly in cold water and served with plain French dressing, or it may be cooked and served the same as spinach.

SMALL EARS OF CORN PICKLED.

For this select the very tiny ears of corn; the ears must be sufficiently young for the cob to be easily penetrated with a fork. Take off the husks, remove the silk, throw the ears into boiling water, boil five minutes, drain. To each two dozen cobs allow one quart of cider vinegar, put it in a porcelain-lined kettle, add two bay leaves, a slice of onion, one dozen pepper-corns, a blade of mace, six whole cloves. Bring to boiling point, pour over the cobs; stand aside twenty-four hours and they are ready for use.

By adding two tablespoonfuls of chopped horse-radish, the cobs will keep nicely all winter.

SALTED CORN.

Cut the corn from the cob uncooked. Put a layer in the bottom of a cask, then a layer of salt, another layer of corn, another layer of salt and so continue until the cask is full. Place a board on top of the corn, on which put a heavy stone and keep it below the brine. This cask may be filled at intervals by lifting the board, adding more corn and replacing it. After packing the corn, if you find in two or three days that there is not sufficient moisture to moisten the salt, add about one pint of water. Then as the juice comes from the corn there will be sufficient brine to cover it thoroughly. When the cask is filled, put a few horse-radish tops underneath the board; this will prevent souring and molding. Cover the cask with a cloth, tucking it in closely around the edges. Then put the board over the whole.

I have known corn, if properly packed, to keep perfectly for two years. In the winter this may be cooked and served the same as fresh corn. Of course it must be soaked over night in water to remove the salt. This is by far a more wholesome way of preserving corn than canning.

CORN IN TINS.

Remove the corn from the cob and pack uncooked into small tin cans. Put on the lids and solder in such a way as to hermetically seal. Stand these in a wash boiler, cover with cold water. Cover the boiler and place over the fire where the water will come gradually to a boil. Boil continually an hour and a half. Then take a small ice-pick or needle and puncture the centre of each lid. The hole should be like a pinhole. Allow the gases and steam to escape freely, then drop over the hole just one drop of solder. Be sure you have them thoroughly sealed. Continue the boiling two and a half hours. If this process is strictly adhered to according to directions given, not one can in one hundred will be lost. It is far safer than using the glass jars, although even then there is little difficulty with care.

Lima beans and corn may be mixed, boiled until thoroughly done and canned as directed.

SOUTHERN CORN PUDDING.

Score twelve good sized ears of corn and with a dull knife press out the pulp. Add a teaspoonful of salt, a quarter teaspoonful of pepper and a pint of milk. Beat four eggs separately until very light, add first the yolks, then stir in the whites. Turn the mixture into a baking dish and bake in a quick oven until a nice brown and thoroughly set—that is, when you shake the dish the centre seems firm. If the pudding is cooked too long it becomes curdled and watery; if not long enough, too liquid.

CORN OYSTERS.

Score and press the corn as directed in preceding recipe; to every pint of pulp allow

2 eggs,
2 heaping tablespoonfuls of flour,
½ teaspoonful of salt,
1 dash of cayenne,
1 dash of black pepper.

Beat the eggs separately; add first the yolks and then the whites to the corn, mix gently, add the salt, cayenne, black pepper and flour; mix again. Put two tablespoonfuls of lard or butter in a frying pan; when hot, drop the mixture by spoonfuls into it; when brown on one side, turn and brown the other. Serve very hot.

CORN PUDDING.

1 dozen large ears of young corn,   1 pint of milk,
4 eggs,   1 teaspoonful of salt,
            ¼ teaspoonful of black pepper.

Score the corn down the centre of each row of grains, then with the back of the knife press out all the pulp, leaving the hull on the cob. Beat the whites and yolks of the eggs separately, add the yolks to the corn, mix thoroughly; then add the salt, pepper and milk, and stir in carefully the whites of the eggs. Brush a pudding dish lightly with butter and pour in the mixture. Bake slowly one hour. Serve as an accompaniment to roast beef or lamb.

SUCCOTASH.

1 pint of young lima or kidney   ½ pint of milk or cream,
    beans,   1 tablespoonful of butter,
1 pint of corn pressed from the Salt and pepper to taste.
    cob,

Shell the beans, cover them with boiling water, add a teaspoonful of salt and boil twenty-five minutes; then add an eighth-teaspoonful of baking soda, boil one minute, then drain. Score the corn and press it from the cob, add it to the beans, then add the milk, butter, salt and pepper, stir *continually* over the fire for five minutes, and it is ready to serve.

In winter, when the corn and beans are dried, soak both separately over night. In the morning, cover the beans with fresh water and boil gently for two hours. Do not drain the water from the corn, but keep it on the back part of the fire where it will not boil during the two hours the beans are boiling. When the beans are tender, drain them, add them to the corn, which should have just water enough to cover. Cook slowly for twenty minutes, then add the cream, butter, salt and pepper.

This may also be made from canned corn and beans.

CORN CHOWDER.

1 quart of grated corn,	3 tablespoonfuls of flour,
4 good sized potatoes,	1 pint of milk,
2 medium sized onions,	6 water crackers,
½ pound of bacon or ham,	Yolk of one egg,
1 large tablespoonful of butter,	½ pint of boiling water.

Pare and cut the potatoes and onions into dice. Cut the bacon or ham into small pieces, put it into a frying pan with the onions and fry until a nice brown. Put a layer of potatoes in the bottom of a saucepan, then a sprinkling of bacon or ham and onion, then a layer of corn, then a sprinkling of salt and pepper, then a layer of potatoes and so on, until all is in, having the last layer corn. Now add the water and place over a very moderate fire and *simmer* for twenty minutes. Then add the milk. Rub the butter and flour together and stir into the boiling chowder. Add the crackers, broken; stir; and cook five minutes longer. Taste to see if properly seasoned, take it from the fire, add the beaten yolk of the egg and serve.

STEWED CUCUMBERS.

6 cucumbers,	1 tablespoonful of butter,
1 tablespoonful of flour,	1 small onion,
½ pint of stock,	Salt and pepper to taste.

Pare the cucumbers, cut into quarters, remove the seeds. Put the butter in a frying pan, add the onion sliced, fry until brown; then add the cucumbers, shake them carefully until they are a light brown, then take them out carefully with an egg-slice. Add the flour to the butter remaining in the pan, mix until smooth; add the stock, stir continually until it boils, then add salt and pepper to taste. Return the cucumbers, cover and stew gently twenty minutes; serve on squares of buttered toast. These may be served with roasted chicken or baked fish.

CUCUMBERS WITH CREAM SAUCE.

6 cucumbers,
1 tablespoonful of flour,
½ pint of milk,
Salt and pepper to taste,
2 tablespoonfuls of butter.

Pare the cucumbers, cut into quarters, remove the seeds, lay them in cold water for thirty minutes. Then put them in a saucepan, cover with boiling water, add a teaspoonful of salt, boil thirty minutes. When done, lift them carefully with a skimmer and place them in a vegetable dish. Put half the butter in a saucepan; when melted, add the flour, mix until smooth, add the milk; stir continually until it boils, add the salt and pepper, take from the fire. Stir in the remaining quantity of butter, pour over the cucumbers and serve garnished with squares of fried bread.

STUFFED CUCUMBERS.

Cut each cucumber in halves and scrape out the seeds. To each six allow a half cup of bread crumbs, two tablespoonfuls of chopped ham, one tablespoonful of parsley, one tablespoonful of chopped onion, salt and pepper to taste. Mix the ingredients together, fill the cucumbers, tie the two halves together, place them in a baking pan. Add one cup of water to the pan, cover with another pan and bake in a moderate oven three-quarters of an hour. Serve with drawn butter in a boat. The cucumbers may also be served in halves and the sauce poured over them.

FRIED CUCUMBERS.

Pare the cucumbers, cut them in slices about a quarter of an inch thick, season with salt and pepper. Dip first in egg, then in bread crumbs. Put two tablespoonfuls of lard or dripping in a frying pan with salt. Put in a few slices of cucumber, fry brown and crisp on one side, then turn and fry brown on the other. Lift carefully, drain on brown paper, serve very hot with tomato catsup.

CUCUMBERS FRIED IN BATTER.

Pare the cucumbers, cut into slices about a sixteenth of an inch thick. Dredge them with salt and pepper. Beat one egg until light, add to it a half pint of milk, a half teaspoonful of salt, a dash of pepper, one and a half cups of sifted flour. Beat until smooth. Dip the pieces of cucumber in this batter and drop, one at a time, into smoking hot fat. The fat must be deep enough to float them. When brown and crisp on one side, turn and fry brown on the other. Lift with a skimmer, as turning with a fork makes them heavy: Drain on brown paper and serve as an accompaniment to boiled or panned steak.

TO SALT CUCUMBERS FOR PICKLING.

Choose very small cucumbers and these as free from spots as possible. Put a layer in the bottom of a cask, then a layer of coarse salt, Liverpool is best. The layer of salt should be at least a quarter of an inch thick. On this put another layer of cucumbers, another of salt and so continue until all the cucumbers are used. Place a board on top of the pickles, on which put a heavy stone to keep them down. If you gather the cucumbers from your own garden, do so as early in the morning as possible or late in the evening. I have known the cutting of cucumbers at midday to entirely ruin the vines. When twenty-five or thirty small cucumbers are packed, add a half pint of water to moisten the salt; this, with the juice of the cucumbers that exudes, will make sufficient brine. If you wish to add a new supply of cucumbers each day to the cask, simply remove the board and stone and arrange in layers as directed. After the cask is filled, put a thick layer of horse-radish tops underneath the board, then cover the cask with a cloth, tucking it down tightly around the edge. In the winter when the cucumbers are wanted for pickling, carefully lift the cloth with the scum, wash the board, stone and cloth in clear warm water. Do not be alarmed at the heavy scum you may find on top, as this will not injure the cucumbers. Take out as many cucumbers as are wanted, wipe down the sides of the cask, return the board, stone and cloth. Cover closely as before. Put the cucumbers taken out in a large vessel of cold water and soak three days, changing the water each day. At the end of this time drain and wipe each cucumber carefully without bruising. If you have cabbage leaves at hand add three or four good-sized leaves to the pickles while soaking. Put into a porcelain-lined kettle a sufficient quantity of vinegar to cover the cucumbers; stand it over the fire. If you wish the pickles crisp at the expense of health, add a piece of alum the size of a hazel-nut. Let the whole come to a boil; turn the cucumbers several times with a wooden spoon or those at the bottom will become soft and lose their crispness. The cucumbers, understand, must not be *cooked*, but simply made crisp by the heating vinegar. The moment it begins to steam or *simmer* take from the fire, drain the cucumbers and put them in a stone jar. Throw this vinegar away. Cover the cucumbers with fresh, cold vinegar; spices may be added according to taste. A tablespoonful of chopped horse-radish will prevent molding. They will be ready for use in about one week.

SMALL CUCUMBER PICKLES.

Wash and wipe carefully a hundred tiny cucumbers, place them in jars. Put sufficient water in a porcelain-lined kettle to cover the cucumbers. When the water is boiling hot stir in enough salt to make a brine that will bear an egg. Pour this boiling brine over the cucumbers. Let them stand twenty-four hours, then take them out, wipe each carefully without bruising, place them in clean jars. Put sufficient vinegar in a porcelain kettle to cover them, add one onion sliced, twelve whole cloves, one ounce of mustard seed, three blades of mace. Let these come to boiling point, pour over the pickles, add two tablespoonfuls of chopped horse-radish, stand aside to cool. They will be ready to use in two weeks and will keep all winter.

OILED PICKLES.

100 small cucumbers,
1 teaspoonful of black pepper,
1 quart of onions,
1 ounce of celery seed,
¼ pound of ground mustard,
¼ pound of whole mustard,
1 pint of olive oil,
2 quarts of cider vinegar.

Pare the cucumbers and onions and cut them into thin slices. Put in a layer of cucumbers, then a layer of onions, then a layer of cucumbers and so continue until all have been used. Cover with a cold brine sufficiently strong to bear an egg, stand aside over night. In the morning drain, cover them with cold water, soak two hours and drain again. Put them in a porcelain-lined kettle with sufficient cold vinegar to cover them; stand them over a fire until the vinegar is lukewarm, then stand away over night; drain. This vinegar may be saved for other purposes, but cannot be used for the pickles. Now put the cucumbers and onions in glass quart jars. Mix the mustard, pepper and celery seed with the oil; then add; gradually stirring all the while, two quarts of cider vinegar. Pour this over the cucumbers and onions, fasten the jars and in two weeks the pickles will be ready for use and will keep all winter.

CUCUMBER CATSUP.

Pare and remove the seeds from two large, ripe cucumbers, then grate them. Drain this pulp in a colander; there should be enough to measure one pint after all the juice is thoroughly drained away. Turn it into an earthen boiler; add a quarter of a teaspoonful of cayenne, a half pint of cider vinegar, one teaspoonful of salt, two heaping tablespoonfuls of grated horse-radish; bottle and seal. Serve with cold meats.

It is especially nice with cold corned beef.

SWEET PICKLED CUCUMBERS.

Pare and cut in thick slices six good sized cucumbers; weigh and to each seven pounds allow four pounds of sugar and one pint of cider vinegar, twelve whole cloves, quarter of an ounce of stick cinnamon, two blades of mace.

Put the sugar, vinegar and spices on to boil in a porcelain kettle; add the cucumbers to this, stand them over a very moderate fire, turning them carefully until each piece seems thoroughly cooked but not soft. Stand aside until morning; next day bring them again to a boiling point and stand aside to cool. Do this also the next morning. Then lift the cucumbers carefully, place them in jars; boil the liquor down until the quantity is just sufficient to cover them. Pour this over hot, fasten the jars and stand in a cool, dry place to keep.

CUCUMBER MANGOES.

12 large cucumbers,	1 root of horse-radish,
1 onion,	1 small head of cabbage,
¼ ounce of cloves,	¼ ounce of ginger,
1 teaspoonful of mace,	2 ounces of whole mustard seed,
1 tablespoonful of salt.	

Select the largest cucumbers you can find, but take them before they are too ripe or have yellow ends. Cut long, narrow pieces out of the sides of each and with a spoon scoop out the seeds. Chop the cabbage fine, add all the spices and seasoning to it. Fill the cucumbers with this mixture, put the piece into the side and tie it with twine. Put the cucumbers into a stone jar, cover with cold vinegar, add the horse-radish chopped fine, and in one week they will be ready for use. A few hot peppers placed here and there among the cucumbers improve the flavor.

If the cucumber mangoes become flat or tasteless, drain off the vinegar and cover with fresh vinegar, adding also fresh horse-radish.

WILTED DANDELIONS.

Cut the roots from a quarter of a peck of young dandelions. Of course these are not fit for food after they are old enough to blossom. Wash the leaves through several cold waters, drain and shake them dry. Take a handful of leaves, cut them with a sharp knife into small pieces and put them in a saucepan. Beat one egg until light, add to it a gill of cream, stir over a fire until it thickens. Add a piece of butter the size of a walnut, two tablespoonfuls of vinegar, salt and pepper to taste. Pour this over the dandelions and stir over the fire just a moment until they are wilted and tender. Serve garnished with little rolls of crisp bacon.

DANDELIONS, (GERMAN STYLE).

Cut the roots from a quarter of a peck of dandelions, wash and cut as directed in the preceding recipe. Cut a quarter of a pound of ham in dice, fry until a golden brown; add one tablespoonful of vinegar. Beat one egg without separating, add to it two tablespoonfuls of cream, stir this quickly in with the ham, add a teaspoonful of onion juice, then the dandelions, stir over the fire one moment and serve very hot.

Dandelions also make a delightful salad. See directions under Salads.

ENDIVE.

The delicate white endive, with French dressing, makes one of the most delightful dinner salads and may also be wilted the same as dandelions.

SOUR OR NARROW DOCK.

This common weed grows along the roadsides or rich pasture fields. The leaves are long, narrow and curly; they may be cooked the same as spinach, but make a much more delicate green. It is supposed to possess alterative properties, forming an excellent diet in scorbutic cases. As it grows early in the spring, long before the ordinary farmer has greens for the table, it makes an excellent accompaniment to the salt meat that is so freely used by them.

FRIED EGG-PLANT.

Pare an egg-plant, cut it into slices a sixteenth of an inch thick. Beat an egg lightly, add to it a tablespoonful of hot water. Dip each slice first into the egg, then into bread crumbs. Put three tablespoonfuls of lard or dripping into a frying pan; when hot cover the bottom with slices of egg-plant. Fry brown on one side, then turn and fry brown on the other; a few slices only should be cooked at a time. As the fat is consumed add more, waiting each time for it to re-heat before putting in the egg-plant. Drain the egg-plant on brown paper and serve very hot with tomato catsup.

EGG-PLANT IN BATTER.

Prepare the egg-plant, cut into slices about a quarter of an inch thick, sprinkle with salt and pepper. Make a batter precisely the same as for cucumbers in batter; dip the egg-plant in the batter and fry the same as for fried egg-plant.

BAKED EGG-PLANT.

Wash the egg-plant, put in a kettle, cover with boiling water and boil about half an hour or until tender. Then take it out, cut it into halves and carefully scrape out the soft portion. Leave the skin unbroken and a wall of sufficient thickness to hold it in position. Chop the egg-plant that you have scraped out, add to it a half cup of crumbs, a large tablespoonful of butter, a half teaspoonful of salt and a palatable seasoning of salt and pepper. Mix well, put back in the skins, sprinkle the top lightly with bread crumbs and put in the oven a few minutes to brown.

DRESSED EGG-PLANT.

Pare the egg-plant, cut into slices, throw them into boiling water, add a teaspoonful of salt and boil twenty minutes. Drain and chop fine. Add to it a large tablespoonful of butter, a level teaspoonful of salt, a dash of pepper, put in a saucepan, stirring continually until boiling hot. Serve in a heated dish.

EGG-PLANT FARCIED.

Take two small egg-plants, cut into halves, scrape out the centre, leaving a wall about one inch thick. Chop the white meat of one cooked chicken, add to it half a cup of bread crumbs, one teaspoonful of onion juice, a half teaspoonful of salt, a tablespoonful of melted butter and a palatable seasoning of pepper. Put this in the centre of the egg-plant, sprinkling a few crumbs over the top. Cut one onion and one carrot into slices; put them in the bottom of a baking pan with a bay leaf, four cloves and a blade of mace. Stand the egg-plant on top, add a quart of stock and bake in a moderate oven one hour, basting from time to time with the stock in the pan. When done serve with Spanish sauce poured over it.

LEEKS.

These may be simply washed, thrown into cold water half an hour and served neatly on a pretty dish, or they may be cut into slices and dressed with French dressing.

STEWED LEEKS.

Trim and wash twenty-four leeks, throw in a kettle of salted, boiling water and boil thirty minutes. Drain, arrange in a heated dish with the bulbs all one way. Put a tablespoonful of butter in a saucepan, when melted add a tablespoonful of flour; mix, and add a half pint of milk. Stir constantly until boiled, add a half teaspoonful of salt and a dash of pepper; pour over the leeks and serve hot.

LENTILS.

These are one of the most important of the leguminous seeds and are valuable for soups, stews and rice dishes in which there is a small allowance of nitrogenous elements.

Wash and soak a pint of lentils over night, in the morning drain, cover with warm, soft water and bring quickly to a boiling point. Boil gently about one hour, drain and cover again with fresh, boiling, soft water. Boil gently until the lentils are tender, about another hour. Press them between the thumb and fingers, if they mash quickly under pressure they are done. Drain in a colander. Put two tablespoonfuls of butter in a saucepan, when melted add the lentils; add one tablespoonful of onion juice, a palatable seasoning of salt and pepper; stir over the fire about fifteen minutes and serve very hot. One or two tablespoonfuls of cream may also be added if liked.

LENTILS WITH RICE.

Boil the lentils as directed in the preceding recipe. Wash one cup of rice, throw it into a large kettle of boiling water and boil rapidly thirty minutes. Drain it in a colander and stand it at the oven door ten or fifteen minutes to dry. Each grain must be swollen, white and free from all stickiness. Put two tablespoonfuls of butter into a frying pan, when melted add one onion cut into thin slices. When the onion is golden brown add the lentils and rice, stir over the fire fifteen minutes, season with salt and pepper; serve very hot.

LENTIL ROLLS.

½ cup of lentils,
½ cup of chopped ham,
12 nice, large vine or cabbage leaves,
½ cup of rice,
½ cup of chopped uncooked chicken,
½ teaspoonful of coriander seed,
Salt and pepper to taste.

Boil the lentils and rice as directed in the preceding recipe and mix the two together. Mix the ham, chicken, coriander seed, salt and pepper together; then mix the rice and lentils. Scald the vine or cabbage leaves, shake them carefully to dry. Put two tablespoonfuls of the mixture in each leaf, roll loosely, folding in the ends. Tie with darning cotton and place each roll as finished in the bottom of a large saucepan. Cover with stock, add a bay leaf, one onion cut in slices and a blade of mace. Cover the saucepan and stew slowly three-quarters of an hour; when done take out carefully with an egg-slice. Remove the strings and arrange the rolls neatly in a flat heated dish. Put one tablespoonful of butter in a saucepan, when melted, add an even tablespoonful of flour, mix till smooth, then add a half pint of the stock in which the rolls were boiled, stir continually until thick and smooth. Add the salt and pepper, take from the fire, add the beaten yolk of an egg and two teaspoonfuls of tarragon vinegar. Pour this over the rolls and serve.

This may be served for lunch or as a course by itself.

LETTUCE.

All varieties of lettuce are used principally as salads, but the crisp, green leaves make a delightful garnish for cold meats, boned chicken or vegetable salads.

CABBAGE LETTUCE WITH GRAVY.

Take four full cabbage lettuces, trim off the loose outside leaves, throw the heads into boiling water five minutes, then drain and press them gently to press out the water. Cut them in halves and arrange neatly on a dish, sprinkle with salt and pepper, tie the two halves together. Stand them in a saucepan, cover with one quart of water. Add about one pound of beef, or any fresh meat or pieces of meat left over will answer, add one onion, one blade of mace and a bay leaf; cover the kettle and cook gently one hour. When done, lift carefully with a skimmer, cut the string and arrange the halves neatly on a dish, giving to each piece an oval and compact look. Lightly press it together with a spoon. Put one tablespoonful of butter in a saucepan, add a tablespoonful of flour; boil rapidly the stock in which they were cooked until reduced to one pint; add this to the butter and flour, stir continually until it boils. Strain over the lettuce leaves and serve garnished with squares of toasted bread.

DUTCH LETTUCE.

Wash carefully two cabbage lettuces, separate the leaves and tear each leaf into about three pieces. Cut a quarter of a pound of ham or bacon into dice and fry until brown; while hot add two tablespoonfuls of vinegar. Beat one egg until light, add two tablespoonfuls of sour cream and stir into the ham. Stir this over a fire until it thickens and pour it while hot over the lettuce. Mix carefully with a fork and serve immediately.

BAKED MUSHROOMS.

For baking choose the larger mushrooms; peel, cut the stalks close to the top. Place them upside down in an earthen or porcelain dish, sprinkle with salt and pepper and put a tiny piece of butter in each. Bake in a quick oven twenty minutes; baste two or three times with melted butter. Serve hot on the dish in which they were baked.

BROILED MUSHROOMS.

Peel the large mushrooms, cut off the stalks and dip them in melted butter. Dust them lightly with salt and pepper and let stand in a cool place thirty minutes. Then place them on a broiler top side down; close the broiler very carefully or you will break them into halves. Place them over a clear fire and broil slowly until tender; they should be broiled first on one side, then turned and broiled on the other. Open the broiler carefully, remove the mushrooms with a spoon, place them on small squares of buttered toast. Pour melted butter in the centre of each and serve very hot.

TO STEW CANNED MUSHROOMS.

A can of mushrooms,
1 tablespoonful of flour,
A tablespoonful of sherry,
1 tablespoonful of butter,
Yolk of one egg,
½ pint of milk,
Salt and pepper to taste.

Drain the mushrooms and wash in cold water. Put the butter in a porcelain or granite saucepan, add the mushrooms, stir over the fire about five minutes; dust them with flour, add the milk and stir continually until boiling hot, add the salt and pepper. Take from the fire, add the well-beaten yolk of the egg and the wine, and serve.

In cooking canned mushrooms do not allow them to boil more than five minutes, as they are already cooked, and a second cooking toughens the mushrooms and renders them very indigestible.

MUSHROOMS.

It is highly important for those who employ mushrooms as food, to be able to distinguish those which are edible from the poisonous ones. The edible appear in old sod, in a clear, open, sunny field. They are at first very small on a short foot stalk, and are then known as button mushrooms. Their growth is rapid; in an hour the under skin cracks and the mushroom then opens, spreading like an umbrella, and shows the gills underneath, which should be a pale salmon color. In an hour or so it again changes to a dark brown, and is then called "old." According to M. Richard, even mushrooms which are usually edible may prove poisonous, if collected too late, or in places which are too moist.

The skin of the good mushrooms peels off easily. Those with yellow or white gills, and those which grow in low, damp, shady places, or around decayed stumps of old trees, or any other decayed matter, are to be avoided.

The good mushrooms have invariably an agreeable smell, while the poisonous have a rank, putrid smell. It is always safe to use the canned mushrooms, which are convenient and cheap, but tough and indigestible, and we caution those who eat them to masticate diligently.

It is said that one poisonous mushroom among a pint of good ones, will turn a *silver* spoon black, if stirred with it while they are stewing.

DRIED MUSHROOMS.

Wipe the mushrooms clean, and peel off the skin. Cover the bottoms of shallow baking-pans with white paper, put the mushrooms in a single layer on this, and stand in a cool oven to dry. When dry and shriveled, take them out, put in paper bags, and hang in a cool, dry place.

When wanted for use, put them in cold water or milk, and bring slowly to a *simmer*. In this way they will regain nearly their natural size and flavor.

STEWED MUSHROOMS, No. 1.

Peel the mushrooms, wash them in cold water and cut off the bottom of the stalks. Then put them in a porcelain saucepan; to every pint of mushrooms, add one tablespoonful of butter rolled in flour. Let the mushrooms cook in their own liquor and the butter for fifteen minutes, then add salt and pepper, and serve immediately.

STEWED MUSHROOMS, No. 2.

Peel the mushrooms, wash them in cold water and cut off the bottom of the stalks. Then put them into a porcelain-lined kettle; to every pint of mushrooms add a tablespoonful of butter divided into four bits and rolled in flour. Let the mushrooms cook in their own liquor with the butter and flour for fifteen minutes, then add two tablespoonfuls of thick cream, salt and pepper to taste. Take from the fire, add the well beaten yolk of one egg, and, if you use it, one tablespoonful of sherry. Serve immediately.

MARTYNIAS.

Pick two quarts of martynias. Wipe carefully with a soft cloth, take sufficient cider vinegar to cover, put in a porcelain kettle, add a sliced onion, a dozen whole cloves, two blades of mace, two bay leaves. Put the martynias in a stone jar, pour the vinegar over while hot, add two tablespoonfuls of chopped horse-radish, fasten, and in three or four days they will be ready for use.

OKRA OR GUMBO.

This delightful vegetable is comparatively unknown to many persons living outside of large cities. It is wholesome and nutritious, and seems to be the proper thing to serve with tomatoes or rice. Gumbo soup of the South is a great delicacy, and those who have eaten the Brunswick stew in Virginia will never forget the delicious compound. They may be preserved for winter use by simply cutting them in rings and stringing them on cords to dry, or they may be canned the same as other vegetables.

BOILED OKRA.

Take one quart of young okra, wash well with cold water; put it into a porcelain or granite kettle, as iron always discolors the okra. Put in a half pint of water and a teaspoonful of salt; cover the kettle and *simmer* gently thirty minutes. Then add one tablespoonful of butter, one tablespoonful of vinegar and a dash of pepper. Serve as an accompaniment to roasted or boiled chicken.

OKRA WITH TOMATOES.

1 quart of okra,	1 pint of tomatoes,
1 tablespoonful of butter,	Salt and pepper to taste.

Wash the okra, cut it into thin slices; scald and peel the tomatoes and cut them into small pieces. Put the butter in a porcelain or granite kettle, add a teaspoonful of salt, cover the kettle and *simmer* gently half an hour. Then add the butter and serve very hot.

OKRA WITH RICE.

1 quart of okra,	1 pint of stock,
3 good-sized tomatoes or a pint of stewed tomatoes,	1 onion,
	1 tablespoonful of powdered, dry sassafras leaves (gumbo fillet powder),
1 red pepper,	
1 cup of rice,	
½ pound of ham.	

Wash the okra, cut it into slices. Cut the ham into dice and fry it brown. Peel and cut the tomatoes, put them in a porcelain kettle with the okra, ham, stock, pepper and onion cut into slices. If you can get for this a ginny pepper the dish will be greatly improved. Cover the kettle and *simmer* gently thirty minutes. While this is cooking, wash and boil the rice. When the okra is done, arrange the rice in a mound in the centre of a dish, add the salt, pepper, and sassafras to the okra, boil up once, and pour it around the rice.

This makes a very good and sightly dish. It may be served as a separate course, alone, or as an accompaniment to chicken, mutton or veal.

OKRA FRICASSEED WITH CORN.

Cut one pint of okra into slices. Put two tablespoonfuls of drippings in a frying-pan, put in the okra with one slice of onion and turn till nicely browned, then add one dozen ears of corn scored and pressed out. Stir the corn and watch carefully until thoroughly cooked, about ten minutes. Then drain the contents of the pan to one side. Add to the fat in the pan two tablespoonfuls of flour, mix, add a half pint of milk, stir continually until boiling, add a level teaspoonful of salt and a dash of black pepper. Serve very hot.

STEWED OKRA.

Cut one pint of young okra into slices; slice a good-sized onion, peel and cut in pieces six large tomatoes. Put them in a stewing-pan, add a tablespoonful of butter, teaspoonful of salt and dash of pepper, and a half cup of water. Stew till tender and serve with poultry.

BOILED ONIONS.

1 dozen onions, ½ pint of milk,
1 tablespoonful of flour, 1 tablespoonful of butter,
Salt and pepper to taste.

Remove the skins from the onions and throw them into cold water. If they are very strong, keep them under the water while you remove the skins. Put them into a large saucepan of boiling water, add a teaspoonful of salt, and boil until you can pierce them easily with a fork, about forty minutes. They must be cooked thoroughly but not soft. Then drain them and return to the kettle. Dust them with flour, add the butter, then the milk. Shake them until boiling hot, season and serve. Serve with roasted chicken or turkey.

FRIED ONIONS.

Remove the skins and cut the onions into slices, cover with boiling water, add a teaspoonful of salt and boil twenty minutes. Drain. Put a large tablespoonful of butter in a frying-pan, when hot add the onions, fry thirty minutes, stirring frequently. Add the pepper and salt and serve with broiled or panned steak or fried calves' liver.

BAKED ONIONS.

Choose large, perfect onions, trim the bottoms and remove one or two layers of the outside skin, but do not thoroughly peel them. Throw them in a kettle of boiling water, add a teaspoonful of salt, boil rapidly for about one hour; then drain in a colander. If the onions are large they will not be soft in one hour, if small, cook, of course, a shorter time. Lift each one out separately, dry and roll in squares of tissue paper, twisting tightly at the top to keep it closed. Stand in a baking-pan and bake in a very slow oven one hour. When done, remove the paper, peel the onions, put them in a vegetable dish, pour melted butter over them, dust with salt and pepper and serve with roasted duck, turkey or chicken.

Spanish onions are particularly nice served in this way.

STEWED ONIONS.

Remove the skins from one quart of onions, throw them into cold water, put them in a saucepan, cover with stock and stew slowly one hour if young, two hours if large and old. They must be cooked until tender and soft. When done, drain and turn carefully into a vegetable dish. Put one tablespoonful of butter in a frying-pan, stir until brown; then add one tablespoonful of flour, mix, add a half pint of the stock in which the onions were boiled. Stir continually until it boils, add salt and pepper to taste, pour this over the onions and serve.

STUFFED ONIONS.

Boil six large onions without peeling for one hour. Drain, remove the skins, and with a sharp knife cut out the centre of each. Mix two tablespoonfuls of finely chopped cooked ham or tongue with a half cup of bread crumbs; pour over this one tablespoonful of melted butter, one tablespoonful of cream, a half teaspoonful of salt, and a dash of pepper. Fill the onions with this mixture, place them in a baking-pan, baste them with melted butter, dust them with bread crumbs, and bake in a slow oven one hour. Serve with cream sauce poured over them.

This is one of the most delightful ways of cooking onions, and they may be served with poultry, roasted or braised, or as a garnish for hot beef à la mode.

SCALLOPED ONIONS.

Peel twelve good-sized onions and boil them one hour, drain and cut them into small pieces. Put a layer in the bottom of a baking-dish, sprinkle over them a layer of crumbs, then a sprinkling of cheese and a few bits of butter. Put in another layer of onions, crumbs, cheese, and so continue until the dish is full. Have the last layer crumbs. Put bits of butter over the top, add a half cup of cream, dust with salt and pepper and bake in a moderate oven one hour.

ONIONS GLAZED.

Peel twelve good-sized onions, throw them in boiling water, boil twenty minutes. Drain and throw them into cold water, peel off the first two skins; scrape out the middle of the onion with a teaspoon, making a well about the size of a hickory nut. Put an ounce of butter in a frying-pan, stand the onions bottom side down in the butter. Put a half teaspoonful of sugar in each onion and cook slowly over a fire until soft and slightly colored. Do not allow the butter to burn. Add a half pint of stock, cover the pan and let them cook slowly until the stock is reduced to the consistency of molasses. Baste the onions constantly with this liquor until they are thoroughly glazed, and they are ready to use as a garnish for roast beef or broiled steak, or are frequently served as a garnish to baked rabbits.

ONION OR SAUCE SOUBISE.

Peel and cut in slices three large onions. Put them into a saucepan with one ounce of butter, cover, and *simmer* gently about three-quarters of an hour; the onions must be colored. When tender and soft, add a tablespoonful of flour, mix and press through a colander. Add one gill of stock and one gill of cream, stir continually until it boils. Add a half teaspoonful of salt, a dash of pepper, a grating of nutmeg and it is ready to serve.

ONION VINEGAR.

1 quart of cider vinegar,   2 large Spanish onions or 4 ordi-
2 teaspoonfuls of white sugar,   nary white onions,
1 teaspoonful of salt.

Peel and grate the onions, mix with them the salt and sugar. Let it stand two hours and add the vinegar. Turn into bottles and shake every day for two weeks. Strain through cheese-cloth, bottle and cork.

This may be used for salads or may be added to French dressing instead of plain vinegar, and may be used in stews or other dishes where a very delicate onion flavor is desired.

PICKLED ONIONS.

Peel the small white button onions, and pour over them boiling brine that is sufficiently strong to bear an egg. Let it stand twenty-four hours, drain and put in bottles. Take sufficient vinegar to cover the onions, add spices to taste, and pour over the onions boiling hot. When cool fasten, and they will be ready to use in four or five days and will keep all winter. If the slightest mould appears on the surface, drain off the vinegar and cover with fresh, hot vinegar.

PARSNIPS BOILED, WITH CREAM SAUCE.

If they are young and tender scrape them and throw each as soon as finished into cold water, to prevent discoloration. If old they must be pared and cut into quarters lengthwise. Put them in a saucepan of boiling water and boil till tender. If young, three-quarters of an hour, if old, one hour and a quarter will be needed. When tender, drain, put on a heated dish heads all one way; cover with Cream Sauce or English drawn butter and serve with corned beef or boiled salt fish.

FRIED PARSNIPS.

Boil as directed in preceding recipe; when done, drain, season with salt and pepper, dip first in melted butter, then in flour and dust with sugar. Put two tablespoonfuls of drippings or lard into a frying-pan, when hot, put in enough parsnips to cover the bottom of the pan. Fry brown on one side, then turn and brown on the other. Serve with roasted pork.

PARSNIP FRITTERS.

4 good-sized parsnips, 1 tablespoonful of flour,
1 egg.

Boil the parsnips until tender, when done, drain and mash through a colander. Add the flour and well-beaten egg, a half teaspoonful of salt and a dash of pepper. Mix well and form into small, round cakes. Put two tablespoonfuls of drippings into a frying pan, when hot put in the cakes. Brown on one side, then turn and brown on the other. Drain on brown paper and serve with roasted or spiced beef.

BAKED PARSNIPS.

6 good-sized parsnips, 1 tablespoonful of butter.
1 tablespoonful of flour, ½ teaspoonful of salt,
Dash of pepper.

Wash and scrape the parsnips, cut them in halves; put them into a saucepan, cover with boiling water and boil one hour. Drain, and put them on a hot dish. Put the butter in a frying-pan, add to it the flour, mix until smooth without browning. Add a half pint of the water in which the parsnips were boiled, stir and boil five minutes. Add the salt and pepper, pour over the parsnips, dust with crumbs, and if liked, a little cheese. Bake in a quick oven fifteen minutes.

GREEN PEAS.

Peas, like corn, lose their sweetness very quickly after picking. If necessary to keep them over night, they should be spread out on a cloth on a cool cellar floor. If, however, you should be so unfortunate as to get stale or wilted peas, they should be shelled at once, thrown into cold water at least one hour before cooking, and then a teaspoonful of sugar should be added to the water in which they are boiled. This artificial flavoring will only partly restore the flavor of the peas. Fresh peas, however, should not be shelled until just before cooking. They should then be washed quickly in cold water, thrown in a kettle of salted boiling water, and boiled ten or fifteen minutes. Long boiling cracks the skins and destroys the color and flavor of the peas. When tender, drain, turn into a hot dish, add a lump of butter. Dust with salt and pepper and serve at once.

The most important point in cooking peas is to have plenty of water. The water must be slightly salted and the peas boiled just long enough to become tender, and drained at once. In this way they will retain their color and sweetness. There are many varieties of peas, many of which are coarse and only fit for drying. The choice kinds of garden peas are, of course, sweet, nutritious and wholesome. There is also a kind of pea called sugar pea, the pods of which are gathered young and cooked and eaten with the seeds in, the same way as we use string beans. Boiled, and dressed with butter, salt and pepper, they are delicious.

If peas are old or have been picked some time before cooking, it is very difficult to make them tender. Indeed, the longer they are boiled, the harder they become. In this condition they are not digestible. It is best to save them for another meal, and by pressing them through a sieve they may be made into a palatable and digestible soup.

TO CAN PEAS.

Fill glass jars full of uncooked peas, then pour in sufficient cold water to fill to the very top, and lay the tops on the jars. Place straw or hay in the bottom of a wash boiler; place the jars on this, or better still, stand in a wire frame. Pour around sufficient cold water to half cover the jars. Put the boiler over a moderate fire, cover closely with the lid and boil steadily three hours. Lift out the jars, see that each is filled with boiling water to overflowing, screw on the covers as tightly as possible, stand aside, where the air will not strike them, to cool. When cold, again screw the covers, wipe the jars, and place them in a *dark*, cool, dry place. If the peas shrink in cooking, it is well to empty one jar to fill the others.

OMELET WITH PEAS.

Boil one cup of shelled peas in salt water fifteen minutes. Drain, and keep hot while you make an omelet.

Beat four eggs without separating until well mixed, add to it four tablespoonfuls of warm water, a piece of butter the size of a walnut and about four drops of onion juice. Put another piece of butter the same size in a perfectly smooth frying-pan; when the butter is hot turn in the eggs. Shake over a quick fire until the eggs are set. Lift one side of the omelet, allowing the soft portion to run underneath, dust with salt and pepper. Put two tablespoonfuls of cooked peas in the centre of the omelet, fold one-half over the other and turn it out on a heated dish. Season the remaining quantity of peas, add one tablespoonful of melted butter to them. Pour around the omelet and serve at once. This makes an exceedingly nice entrée at dinner or a nice dish for supper or lunch.

TO COOK CANNED PEAS.

After opening the can drain the peas, throw them into cold water and drain again in a colander. Put them in a saucepan, and to each pint can allow one tablespoonful of butter, a half teaspoonful of salt and a dash of pepper. Shake gently until they are thoroughly hot and serve at once.

PEAS WITH CREAM SAUCE.

Put one quart of peas in a kettle of salted, boiling water and cook fifteen minutes; drain. Put a tablespoonful of butter in a saucepan, add a tablespoonful of flour, mix. Add a half pint of milk, stir continually until boiling; add a half teaspoonful of salt, a dash of pepper and then the peas. Stand over boiling water about five minutes and serve as a garnish to baked, broiled or fried sweetbreads or squabs.

SUGAR PEA PODS.

Select young, tender pods, wash them in cold water, throw them in a kettle of boiling water, add a teaspoonful of salt and boil thirty minutes. Drain, turn into a heated dish, pour over Cream Sauce and serve; or they may be served with butter, salt and pepper.

These are also nice boiled and put with mixed pickles.

PEPPER MANGOES.

Cut the tops from one dozen red and one dozen green peppers, and if you have them, from one dozen sweet peppers. Remove the seeds, save the tops. Stand the peppers upright in a tub, put one teaspoonful of salt in each, cover with cold water. Soak over night. In the morning drain, and wash well in cold water. Cut three good-sized, hard heads of cabbage on a slaw cutter, add to it one teaspoonful of ground allspice, a half cup of mustard seeds, two tablespoonfuls of salt, and, if liked, one teaspoonful of ground mace. Mix thoroughly and stuff the mixture in the peppers. Put on the tops and tie with soft twine. Stand upright in stone jars, cover with cold vinegar. Stand aside one week; drain off the vinegar. Cover with fresh cold vinegar. Add one cup of nasturtiums or two tablespoonfuls of chopped horse-radish.

PICKLED PEPPERS.

Take one dozen large, green peppers, six red peppers, six yellow sweet peppers. Make a small incision at one side and carefully remove the seeds without breaking the peppers. Make brine sufficiently strong to float an egg. Pour over the peppers and stand aside over night. Next morning drain, and wash carefully in cold water. Put one quart of vinegar in a porcelain kettle, bring to boiling point, pour over the peppers and stand aside to cool. When cold, drain, throw this vinegar away. If the vinegar is very strong, add an equal quantity of cold water. Take sufficient fresh vinegar to cover the peppers, bring to boiling point, pour this over the peppers, and when cold put them away for use.

These are nice to mix with cabbage for pepper sauce during the winter.

PEPPER SAUCE.

Chop one red and one green pepper fine. Cut one hard head of cabbage on a slaw cutter. Mix with it two tablespoonfuls of whole mustard seed, one tablespoonful of whole allspice, one tablespoonful of cloves and then add the chopped peppers. Add a tablespoonful of salt, mix, and pack in jars. Cover with cold vinegar, stand aside over night and it is ready to use.

Pepper sauce is much better freshly made. It is not good over four days old.

TO PICKLE CAPSICUMS.

Pick the capsicums just as they are turning red. Make a slit in the sides of each, take out the seeds, throw them into salt and water two days. Drain, put them in glass jars, cover with cold vinegar, cork and stand in a cool place.

They will keep for several years, and as the vinegar is used off cover with fresh vinegar. They may be added to sauces or salads.

STUFFED PEPPERS.

For this use the sweet Spanish peppers, and to each six allow a half pint of chopped cooked chicken, a half pint of stale bread crumbs, a level teaspoonful of salt and a salt spoonful of pepper, a tablespoonful of chopped parsley, two tablespoonfuls of butter.

Cut off the stem end of the peppers and remove the seeds. Throw them in a saucepan of boiling water and cover; stand on the back of the stove fifteen minutes. Mix all the ingredients together except the butter. Melt it and pour over after you have everything thoroughly mixed. Drain the peppers, fill with the stuffing, sprinkle the tops with bread crumbs. Put here and there bits of butter, stand in a baking-pan, and bake in a quick oven fifteen minutes. Serve with roasted beef.

POKE STALKS.

In the spring the young shoots of poke are much used as food. They should never be taken over three inches long, and should show only a small tuft of leaves at the top. Older or larger than this they are poisonous. Wash thoroughly in cold water one hour, tie in bundles like asparagus, put into a kettle of boiling water, add a teaspoonful of salt and boil three-quarters of an hour. Put them on buttered toast after draining, heads all one way. Cover with drawn butter and serve.

POTATOES.

Potatoes, one of the most important of vegetables, are served in nearly every household every day, and out of every ten plates that go to the table only one is really perfect. In the winter when potatoes are crisp and fresh they should be put on to boil in boiling water, but in the spring of the year, when soft and wilted, they should be soaked in cold water and then put to cook in cold water. Sprouts grow at the expense of the starch. The potatoes are not so nutritious and are much harder to cook mealy and palatable. Salt should not be added to potatoes until they are boiled and drained. It then assists in absorbing the moisture, and the potato will become dry and mealy.

As the nutritious part lies near the skin, peel as thin as possible and throw each potato into cold water as soon as pared. Select potatoes of the same size for cooking, all the large potatoes should be cooked at one time, medium sized at another, and the small ones at another. As the starch cells are thicker around the outside, the cutting of a large potato to make it correspond in size to the smaller ones, allows the water to penetrate and the potato becomes sodden and heavy. Potatoes boiled in their jackets are without doubt better than those that are pared. The saline constituents of the potato are potash, and when potatoes are pared a large percentage of these salts, which are freely soluble in water, are drawn out into the water, and the potato has rather a flat taste. This also contradicts the idea of a simple paring around the potato. The salts dissolve out if the skin is broken.

The temperature of boiling water is 212° Fahrenheit under ordinary atmospheric pressure. If the water boils slowly the potatoes will cook just as quickly as though it were boiling at a gallop; and the outside will not be boiled soft and to pieces while the inside is under done. Where the potatoes are large, the boiling may be checked for a moment just before the potatoes are done, and the inside then will be soft as well as the outside.

Potatoes require to be cooked to render them palatable and digestible. This cooking may be either by boiling, baking, steaming or frying, but frying potatoes is the most indigestible way of cooking them. Potatoes that have been once boiled and then fried, unless they are fried carefully in butter, are the most unwholesome and indigestible of foods. Boiled potatoes are almost as difficult of digestion. Steaming is perhaps a better method of cooking than boiling, but baking is better than either of the above methods. Young potatoes, which may be in the early spring more tempting than old ones, are by far more indigestible.

BOILED POTATOES.

Peel the potatoes, throw them into cold water, then put them in a kettle and cover with boiling water. Do not give them a tremendous bath, simply cover them. Put on the lid of the kettle and boil slowly until the potatoes are soft enough to admit a fork easily. This will take about thirty minutes. Remember, if you allow the potatoes to remain in the water one moment after they are done, they become waxy and heavy, and nothing you can do will restore them to their mealy condition. The moment they are tender, drain them, sprinkle with salt, stand on the back part of the range uncovered, giving them an occasional tossing. In a few moments the potato will be mealy and dry, the outside starch cells shining like silver. All varieties and even potatoes not strictly first-class, if treated in this manner, will be comparatively good.

SCALLOPED POTATOES.

Cut cold, boiled potatoes in dice. To every quart of dice allow two tablespoonfuls of butter, two even tablespoonfuls of flour, one pint of milk, one teaspoonful of salt, a quarter of a teaspoonful of pepper.

Put the butter in a saucepan to melt, add the flour, mix until smooth, add the milk, stirring constantly until it boils. Add the salt and pepper and mix the whole carefully with the potatoes. Turn them into a baking-dish, cover the top thickly with stale bread crumbs, put a few bits of butter here and there and bake in a quick oven until a golden brown. Serve in the dish in which they are cooked.

STEAMED POTATOES.

Wash and scrub the potatoes, place them in a steamer, or without a steamer, place them in a colander over a kettle of boiling water. Cover and steam about thirty-five or forty minutes, or until you can pierce them readily with a fork. Allow ten minutes longer for steaming than for boiling potatoes of equal size. When done, remove the skins quickly and serve in an uncovered dish.

In fact, plain boiled or steamed potatoes should be served in a napkin in a potato bowl.

MASHED POTATOES.

Boil as directed for plain boiled potatoes. When done mash quickly in a vegetable press or use a wire masher. To each six potatoes allow a piece of butter the size of a walnut, one gill of boiled milk or cream, a teaspoonful of salt and a dash of pepper. Beat with a wooden fork till very light. Serve in a heated, uncovered dish.

POTATO CROQUETTES.

2 cups plain mashed potatoes,	2 tablespoonfuls of cream,
1 teaspoonful of onion juice,	1 teaspoonful of salt,
Grating of nutmeg,	Yolks of two eggs,
1 tablespoonful of chopped parsley,	Piece of butter the size of a walnut,

Dash of cayenne.

Beat the yolks, add the potatoes and then add all the other ingredients, mix, and turn into a small saucepan. Stir over the fire until the mixture leaves the sides of the pan. Take from the fire and when cool, form into small cylinders. Beat an egg without separating, add to it a tablespoonful of warm water. Dip the cylinders first in this and then into bread crumbs, and fry in smoking hot fat. Potato croquettes are the hardest of all croquettes to fry. If the covering cracks, allowing the potatoes to escape, the fat is not sufficiently hot or the covering has not been put on perfectly. See that the ends are thoroughly covered with both egg and bread crumbs. The quantity given will make twelve croquettes. Cold mashed potatoes may be used.

POTATO PUFF.

2 cups of mashed potatoes,　　3 tablespoonfuls of cream,
2 eggs,　　1 tablespoonful of butter,
Salt and pepper to taste.

Put the potatoes in a saucepan, add the yolks, cream, and seasoning, stirring constantly over the fire until the potatoes are very light and hot. Take from the fire and stir in carefully the well-beaten whites of the eggs. Put the potatoes carefully in a greased baking dish, or into small gem pans. Bake in a quick oven until brown.

BOULETTES OF POTATO.

2 cups of mashed potatoes,　　Yolks of two eggs,
2 tablespoonfuls of cream,　　1 teaspoonful of powdered sweet
1 teaspoonful of onion juice,　　marjoram,
Piece of butter the size of a walnut,　　1 tablespoonful of chopped parsley,
Salt and pepper to taste.

Beat the yolks lightly, add the potatoes, then add all the other ingredients. Mix well, put them in a saucepan, and stir over the fire until the mixture leaves the sides of the pan. Take from the fire. When cold, form into bullets. Dip first in egg then into bread crumbs and fry in smoking hot fat. Use as a garnish to boiled or baked fish.

STEWED POTATOES.

Pare six potatoes and cut into dice. Throw them into cold water fifteen minutes. Drain, cover with boiling water and boil ten minutes after they begin to boil. Then drain off every drop of water, put the potatoes in a double boiler, dredge with a tablespoonful of flour, add a tablespoonful of butter, half a pint of milk; cover and cook gently fifteen minutes. Season with salt and pepper and serve in a heated dish.

POTATOES WITH CREAM SAUCE.

Prepare the potatoes as directed for stewed potatoes. After they are drained turn into a heated dish, pour over the Cream Sauce, sprinkle with chopped parsley and serve.

POTATOES au GRATIN.

½ pint of milk,
Yolks of four eggs,
2 tablespoonfuls of butter,
6 boiled potatoes,
1 tablespoonful of flour,
½ pint of stock,
4 tablespoonfuls of grated cheese,
Salt and cayenne to taste.

Cut the potatoes into slices and put them into a baking-dish. Put the butter in a saucepan to melt, add the flour, mix, add the stock and cream, stir continually until they boil; take from the fire, add the cheese, the yolks, well beaten, salt and cayenne. Pour this over the potatoes, sprinkle bread crumbs over the top, put in a quick oven ten minutes to brown. Serve in the dish in which they were baked with duck, roasted wild turkey, mutton or game.

HASHED BROWNED POTATOES.

Chop two cold boiled potatoes fine, dust with salt and pepper. Put a tablespoonful of butter in a frying-pan, when hot put in the potatoes. Spread them out perfectly even and about half an inch in thickness. Stand the pan over a moderate fire and cook slowly without stirring for about fifteen minutes. Then begin at one side of the pan and roll over carefully as for an omelet. Pack or bank the potatoes against one side of the pan. Take a small meat dish, place it against the side of the pan, turn the pan over, turning out the potatoes on to the dish in a roll nicely browned over the outside. Considerable practice is required before one can manage the roll without breaking.

HASHED POTATOES WITH CREAM.

Chop fine four cold boiled potatoes, put them in a saucepan with a half pint of cream, half a teaspoonful of salt, dash of pepper, grating of nutmeg and two ounces of butter. Shake over a fire until very hot and serve at once.

After these are very hot they may be turned into a baking-dish, dusted with bread crumbs and baked in a quick oven until golden brown, and are then called Delmonico potatoes.

HASHED BROWNED POTATOES IN THE OVEN.

Cut into dice four good-sized cold boiled potatoes, put them in a baking-dish and just cover with cream. Add a teaspoonful of butter cut into bits and bake in a moderate oven about thirty minutes. Serve in the dish in which they are baked. These are delicious served with broiled or panned steak.

PANNED POTATOES.

Chop fine two uncooked potatoes, put them in a shallow baking-dish. Add two ounces of butter, a half teaspoonful of salt, and a dash of pepper. Cover with crumbs and bake them in a moderate oven three-quarters of an hour.

FRENCH FRIED POTATOES.

Pare six good-sized potatoes and throw them into cold water. Then with a potato scoop, scoop out into little round balls. This scoop may be purchased at a hardware store for twenty-five cents. Throw these balls into boiling water, boil five minutes, drain. Then put them in a frying-pan a few at a time. Sink them in a pan of smoking hot fat and fry a golden brown. When done, drain, sprinkle with salt and serve as a garnish to boiled or baked fish, or serve plain for breakfast.

POTATO SAUTÉS.

Cut cold boiled potatoes into dice; to each good-sized potato allow a tablespoonful of butter. Put it in a frying-pan; when hot put in the potatoes, a few at a time. Never put in more than will nicely cover the bottom of the pan. Stir carefully and cook the potatoes a golden brown. Dust with salt and pepper, turn into a heated dish and serve hot.

LYONNAISE POTATOES.

Cut two cold boiled potatoes into dice. Put a tablespoonful of butter in a frying-pan. When hot, add one onion sliced; stir until the onion is a golden brown. Add the potatoes, cook slowly until the potatoes are lightly colored, sprinkle with salt. Turn into a hot dish, sprinkle with chopped parsley and serve. These are exceedingly nice served with broiled steak, fried chicken or fried liver.

POTATOES, à la HOLLANDAISE.

Peel six good-sized potatoes and cut them in balls with a potato scoop. Throw the balls in boiling water and boil five minutes. When done, drain, put in a saucepan, add two tablespoonfuls of butter, put them on the back part of the range, shaking occasionally until the potatoes absorb the butter entirely and they are thoroughly tender. Turn into a hot dish, pour over Sauce Hollandaise and serve with baked or boiled fish.

POTATOES, à la DUCHESSE.

2 cups of mashed potatoes,   2 tablespoonfuls of butter,
2 eggs,   1 teaspoonful of salt,
1 teaspoonful of sugar.

Add the butter, salt and sugar to the potatoes, mix and stir till light, then add two eggs well beaten. Form into oval cakes, brush the tops with melted butter. Place them on a greased paper and run them in the oven until the tops are nicely browned. Serve with fricassee of chicken or rabbit.

RAGOUT OF POTATOES.

6 potatoes,   1 tablespoonful of chopped Chervil,
6 leeks,   12 stalks of asparagus,
1 tablespoonful of butter,   ½ pint of milk,
Salt and pepper to taste.

Cut the potatoes in dice, throw them into boiling water, add the leeks cut into slices. Boil ten minutes and drain. At the same time boil and drain the asparagus, but in a separate kettle. Now mix the two together. Put the butter in a saucepan, add the milk and Chervil, salt and pepper, stir carefully over the fire until scalding hot. Pour it over the potatoes, bring to boiling point and serve.

SARATOGA CHIPS.

Pare two large potatoes, cut them into very thin slices lengthwise. Throw them in cold water about one hour; less time will answer perfectly well. When ready to fry take out a few pieces at a time and dry on a soft towel. Have ready a kettle of smoking lard; put the slices in a frying basket, or you can throw them into the fat, lift and stir with a skimmer; when light brown take out, place on a soft brown paper in a colander, dredge with salt and stand in the oven to keep warm while you fry the remainder. These may be served for breakfast or as a garnish for broiled steak or chops.

BAKED POTATOES.

As potatoes contain potash, an important constituent of the blood, freely soluble in water, they are much more wholesome and easily digested baked than boiled, and should always be given to invalids or dyspeptics in this form.

Wash and scrub the potatoes, place them in a baking-pan, then in a quick oven to bake thirty minutes. The time depends on the size of the potatoes, but bake until they mash gently between the thumb and finger. Do not try them by piercing with a fork, as this breaks the skin and allows the steam to escape and the potato will be heavy and watery. Cold baked potatoes left over may be made into stuffed potatoes and put away for another meal, but they must be stuffed while warm and then baked when needed.

STUFFED POTATOES.

6 good-sized potatoes,	1 tablespoonful of butter,
1 gill of hot milk,	1 teaspoonful of salt,
2 eggs,	Dash of pepper.

Bake the potatoes till done, then cut in halves and with a spoon scrape out the potato into a hot bowl. Leave sufficient potato in the skins to keep them in shape. Mash the potato fine, add the butter, hot milk, salt and pepper. Beat until very light, then stir in carefully the well-beaten whites of eggs. Fill the skins with this mixture, heaping them up. Brush over with yolk of egg and put in the oven till golden brown.

POTATOES BAKED WITH MEAT.

Wash and pare potatoes of uniform size, and one hour before the meat is done put the potatoes into the baking-pan, around it. Baste them with the dripping every time you baste the meat. Turn them once or twice. Potatoes cooked in this way are palatable but rather difficult to digest.

POTATO CHOWDER.

6 good-sized potatoes,
1 good-sized onion,
1 tablespoonful of chopped parsley,
1 tablespoonful of butter,
¼ pound of bacon or ham,
A pint of milk and a pint of water,
1 tablespoonful of flour.

Pare and cut the potatoes in dice. Chop an onion fine. Cut the bacon or ham into small pieces and put it in a frying-pan. Add the onion, cook until a light brown. Put one layer of potatoes in the bottom of a saucepan, then sprinkle over the ham and onion, the parsley, salt and pepper. Then another layer of potatoes, then ham and onion and so continue until all the materials are used. Add the water, cover closely and cook on the back part of the stove twenty minutes. Then add the milk; rub the butter and flour together, then stir carefully into the boiling chowder. Cook one moment, taste to see if properly seasoned and serve very hot.

POTATO SOUFFLÉ.

Steam six good-sized potatoes in their jackets. When done peel and mash them. Add to them while hot one tablespoonful of butter, a half pint of cream, one teaspoonful of salt and pepper to taste. Beat till smooth and light. Beat the whites of the four eggs to a stiff froth, stir gently into the potatoes. Heap them on a baking-dish or drop by spoonfuls on greased paper. Dust with grated cheese and put in a quick oven till a golden brown. Serve hot.

POTATO CASSEROLE.

2 cups of mashed potatoes,   Yolks of four eggs,
1 tablespoonful of butter,   1 gill of cream.

Add the yolks of the eggs, cream and butter to the potatoes and stir over the fire until hot. Beat until very light, add the salt and pepper to taste. Form this mixture in a neat border on a tin sheet or old platter. Brush it over with beaten egg, put in the oven until a golden brown. Fill the space with fricasseed chicken, rabbit, or fricassee of veal, and serve.

POTATOES, à la MAITRE D'HÔTEL.

Boil four good-sized potatoes and cut them into dice. Put them in a saucepan, add a half pint of stock, cook slowly about ten minutes. Season with salt and pepper and turn them into a heated dish. Have ready one tablespoonful of butter, one tablespoonful of chopped parsley and a teaspoonful of lemon juice well rubbed together. Spread this over the potatoes and serve at once. These are nice served with broiled, salt fish.

WHITE POTATO CUSTARD.

Grate four good-sized potatoes into one quart of milk. Beat four eggs without separating until light, add the milk and potato. Add one cup of sugar, a teaspoonful of cinnamon, a grating of nutmeg, or you may add the juice and rind of one lemon. Mix thoroughly, pour into deep pans lined with paste, bake in a quick oven thirty minutes.

WHITE POTATO PIE.

To one cup of mashed potatoes add one pint of milk and the yolks of three eggs, well beaten. Mix and add one cup of sugar and the juice and rind of one lemon. Turn this into a deep dish lined with paste, bake in a quick oven thirty minutes. Beat the whites of the eggs until light, add three tablespoonfuls of powdered sugar and beat white and stiff. Heap this over the pie, put back in the oven a few moments to brown.

SWEET POTATOES.

Sweet potatoes contain less starch and more sugar than whites. They must be cooked in a rather more careful manner. They should be mealy and tender when done, not heavy and sodden.

ROASTED SWEET POTATOES.

Wash and scrub those of a uniform size; do not cut or scratch the skin. Put them in a baking-pan, place them in a hot oven and bake until when pressed with the hands they seem mellow in the centre. Do not pierce them with a fork; serve them in their jackets. Roasted potatoes must, of course, be served at once when taken from the oven, or they become heavy.

BAKED SWEET POTATOES.

Wash and scrub potatoes of a uniform size. Do not break the skins, put them in a kettle of boiling water and boil until, when pierced with a fork, they seem a little hard in the centre. Drain, put them in a baking-pan, run them in a hot oven for about fifteen minutes. In this way the potatoes become mealy and dry. Remove the skins when baked and serve in an uncovered dish.

BROWNED SWEET POTATOES.

After the potatoes have been boiled and dried in the oven, remove the skins and cut into halves. Put three tablespoonfuls of drippings in a large frying-pan. Dust the potatoes with salt, pepper and sugar, put them into the hot fat and turn carefully until browned on both sides. Serve very hot.

MASHED SWEET POTATOES, Southern Style.

Boil dry and skin six good-sized sweets. Mash them fine, add two tablespoonfuls of butter, four tablespoonfuls of sugar, a half teaspoonful of salt, beat until light. Put them into a baking-dish and when there is enough, smooth over the top. Brush with milk, and bake in a moderate oven until a light brown. Serve as a separate course by itself.

SWEET POTATO CROQUETTES.

Boil dry and skin six good-sized sweet potatoes. Mash, add a tablespoonful of butter, a half teaspoonful of salt, a dash of pepper. Mix, form into cylinders, dip first in egg and then in bread crumbs and fry in smoking hot fat. Serve with roast meat, poultry or game.

SWEET POTATO BREAD.

4 roasted sweet potatoes,
1 pint of warm water,
1 tablespoonful of butter,
1 quart of flour,
1 tablespoonful of salt,
½ cup of yeast or ½ a compressed cake.

Put the water in a bowl, add the butter, salt, yeast and flour, beat well and stand in a warm place over night. In the morning bake the sweet potatoes, scoop out with a spoon and press through a sieve into the sponge. Beat well; add one egg and sufficient flour to make a soft dough. Knead lightly, roll out and cut into biscuits. Place these in greased baking-pans and when very light bake in a quick oven twenty-five or thirty minutes. When the biscuits are half done, take from the fire, brush over with white of one egg beaten with two tablespoonfuls of water. Put back in the oven until thoroughly done.

SWEET POTATO PIE.

Boil, skin and mash three good-sized sweets. There should be one pint of it, to which add one pint of milk, three eggs beaten light without separating, half cup of sugar, a teaspoonful of vanilla, or half teaspoonful of cinnamon and a level teaspoonful of ginger.

Mix, pour into deep pie-tins lined with light paste and bake in a moderate oven a half hour.

TO DRY PUMPKINS FOR PIES.

Pare the pumpkin, cut into thin strips and again into slices. Spread out in a thin layer and dry in the hot sun or in a moderate oven. In the winter when wanted for use soak over night in cold water. Cook in the same water until tender and use the same as fresh pumpkin.

PRESERVED PUMPKIN.

Pare off the outer skin and cut the pumpkin in halves. Remove the seeds and divide each half into a number of smaller pieces. Cut or chip these into very small, thin shavings. To each quart of these chips allow one large orange. Shave the orange, rind and all, into thin slices, avoiding the core in the centre. Add the orange to the pumpkin, cover with two quarts of cold water and stand in a cold place over night. In the morning cook slowly until the pumpkin is clear and tender and reduced about one-half. Put into tumblers, fasten and keep in a cool, dark place.

PUMPKIN PRESERVED IN PIECES.

Pare off the outer skin, cut in halves, remove the seeds and divide each half into pieces about two inches square. Put them in a stone jar, add a half cup of salt to every five pounds of pumpkin. Cover with cold water and stand aside five hours, then drain and cover with fresh cold water. Soak two hours, changing the water three or four times. If you wish it crisp at the expense of health, dissolve a teaspoonful of powdered alum in two quarts of boiling water, add to the pumpkin and bring to boiling point. If the alum is omitted, bring the pumpkin to boiling point in the water; drain in a colander. Put two and a half pounds of granulated sugar and one and a half quarts of boiling water in a preserving kettle, boil and skim. When perfectly clear, put in the pumpkin and cook gently until you can pierce it with a wooden skewer or straw. Then lift each piece carefully with a skimmer and place it on a large plate. Stand in the sun two hours to harden. Chip the yellow rind from one large lemon, add to the syrup; add the juice of two lemons and a small piece of ginger root cut in thin slices. Boil ten minutes and stand aside to cool. When the pumpkin rind is hardened and cold, put in glass jars. Bring the syrup again to boiling point, strain it over the pumpkin and when cool, fasten or seal.

PUMPKIN PIE.

Pare and cut the pumpkin in pieces one inch square; put them in a stewing-pan with just enough water to keep the pumpkin from burning. Cover and stew slowly about a half hour or until tender. By this time the water should have entirely evaporated. If it has not, however, lift the lid of the kettle and allow it to evaporate. Press the pumpkin through a colander and add while hot a piece of butter the size of a walnut to each pint of pumpkin. When the pumpkin is cold, add a quarter of a teaspoonful of salt, one pint of milk, a half teaspoonful of ground mace, half a teaspoonful of ground cloves, one teaspoonful of ground ginger. Mix all well together, and add a half cup of sugar. Beat four eggs till light, stir them into the mixture, and stand aside about thirty minutes. Remember these quantities are added to one pint of pumpkin. Line four deep pie plates with good, plain paste. Fill them with the mixture, and bake in a quick oven about thirty-five minutes. If you use liquor, one gill of brandy may be added to the recipe given.

BAKED PUMPKIN.

Cut the pumpkin in halves, then in quarters and remove the seeds, not the rind. Place in a baking-pan rind downwards, and bake in a slow oven until tender. Try it by piercing with a fork. When done, dish the pumpkin neatly on a pretty dish, moisten it with butter and serve. Help it by spoonfuls as mashed potatoes. In mid-winter, a nice sweet pumpkin baked and served is not only an attractive but a palatable dish, to my own taste far better than sweet potatoes.

PUMPKIN WITH SALT MEAT.

Peel the pumpkin, cut into thin slices, arrange in a baking-dish with a space in the middle for one pound of salt pork. The pork should be soaked in cold water over night, scored, and placed in the centre of the dish. Smoked salt pork is better than unsmoked. Sprinkle two tablespoonfuls of brown sugar over the pumpkin, add a cup of water, cover and cook slowly in the oven one hour; then remove the cover and cook one hour longer. As the water evaporates add fresh. This very homely sounding dish is, if well prepared, very appetizing.

RADISHES.

Winter radishes may be simply pared, cut in quarters, and arranged neatly on a pretty shallow dish. Red radishes of the spring should have the roots neatly trimmed, half the top cut and trimmed, leaving little holders at the top. These may be arranged neatly in a glass dish, and served with cracked ice.

The round white radishes and the little button radishes may be served as follows: Cut off the roots close to the radish, then the tops about one inch from the radish, wash clean in cold water, then take a radish in the left hand, holding it by the top. Cut the skin from the top downwards, in several parts, as you cut an orange to remove the skin in sections, but do not detach the skin. Now run the point of the penknife under each little section of skin and loosen it down to the stem of the radish. Throw each radish as finished into a bowl of cold water. After a little practice this operation will be comparatively easy and the radishes will look more like tulips than like ordinary table radishes. Serve in a pretty dish with cracked ice, or use as a garnish for fish cutlets, lobster cutlets, breaded chops, etc. The skin of the radish should be eaten with the flesh, as it contains a substance that helps digest the radish itself.

WINTER RADISHES WITH CREAM SAUCE.

Pare and cut the radishes in slices crosswise. Throw them into boiling water, boil twenty minutes. Turn them into a heated dish, cover with Cream Sauce and serve very hot.

PICKLED RADISH PODS.

Pick two quarts of horse-radish pods. They must be tender, green, and with the seeds just forming. Throw them in brine and stand aside over night. Next day turn them, brine and all, into a porcelain kettle and bring to steaming point. Drain, turn them into a jar, and if not tender and green bring the brine to boiling point and pour over the pods again. Continue doing this till the pods are tender and green. Then drain, put one quart of good cider vinegar in a porcelain kettle, add two blades of mace, one ounce of ginger root in slices, two small red peppers, two tablespoonfuls of chopped horse-radish; bring to boiling point and pour over the pods. Stand aside over night. Next morning drain off the vinegar, bring it to boiling point again and pour over the pods. When cold they may be tied up and kept in a cool dry place.

STEWED RHUBARB.

Wash the rhubarb, cut in pieces about one inch long, do not remove the skin. To every pound of rhubarb allow one pound of granulated sugar, put them together in a porcelain kettle and stand on the back of the fire until the sugar slowly melts. Do not add water. Then bring the kettle forward and boil gently without stirring. As soon as the rhubarb is tender, turn it carefully out to cool.

RHUBARB PIE.

Line a pie dish with good plain paste, wash the tender stalks of rhubarb, but do not peel. Cut them in thin slices, fill the dishes even full and to each pie allow five tablespoonfuls of sugar. Cover the pie with the upper crust, making a hole in the centre to allow the escape of steam. Press the edges tightly together and bake in a quick oven forty-five minutes.

RHUBARB VINEGAR.

For five gallons take about fifteen ordinary stalks of rhubarb. Wash and pound or crush it with a potato masher in the bottom of a strong tub, then add five gallons of cold water, cover and stand aside twenty-four hours. Strain off, and add eight pounds of brown sugar, and a cupful of good yeast or one compressed yeast cake dissolved in a cup of lukewarm water. Stir till the sugar is dissolved, then stand in a warm place over night. In the morning put in a ten-gallon cask, place where the temperature will not fall below 60°. In a month strain off the grounds, return to the cask again and let stand until it becomes vinegar, perhaps two or three weeks.

RHUBARB WINE.

Put twenty-five large stalks of rhubarb in the bottom of a tub, pound and mash with a potato masher. Add ten gallons of cold water, let it stand twenty-four hours, then add fifteen pounds of brown sugar. Stir until the sugar is dissolved. Add one cup of brewers' yeast or two compressed yeast cakes dissolved in a cup of warm water. Strain in a cask, let stand over night, then rack off again. Bottle and put in a cold place.

RICE AS A VEGETABLE.

Wash one cup of rice, sprinkle it carefully in a large kettle of boiling water. Cover and boil rapidly without stirring for twenty minutes. Drain, throw into a bowl of cold water to blanch ten minutes. Drain again in a colander, then stand the colander over a kettle of boiling water. Let it steam ten minutes. Stand at the oven door a few minutes to dry. Sprinkle with salt and serve.

Each grain should be swollen two or three times its original size and no two grains should stick together. Serve with fricassee of veal, or of chicken, or with boiled mutton. Where rice is served as a vegetable, do not serve potatoes in any form at the same time.

BOILED SALSIFY OR OYSTER PLANT.

Wash and scrape one dozen roots of salsify, throw each into cold water to prevent discoloration, as soon as scraped. Throw them into a kettle of boiling water, boil slowly about one hour. Drain, arrange neatly on a plate of buttered toast, cover with Cream Sauce and serve.

SALSIFY FRITTERS.

These are made precisely the same as parsnip fritters.

FRIED SALSIFY.

Scrape and boil one dozen roots of salsify; when done, drain, dust with salt, pepper, sugar, and flour. Put two tablespoonfuls of drippings in a frying-pan, when hot put in the salsify. Turn carefully until brown on all sides. Serve with baked or hot boiled ham.

SPINACH.

Wash a half peck of spinach through several waters, to free it from grit. Pick over carefully, cut off the roots. Wash again, drain by taking up in handfuls, shaking, and pressing out all the remaining water. Put in a kettle, add a cupful of water, stand over the fire and boil without covering about ten minutes. Then drain in a colander, turn into a chopping tray, and chop very fine. It cannot be too fine. Then put in a saucepan with two tablespoonfuls of butter, salt and pepper to taste. Stir until very hot. Have ready at hand a heated dish, arrange it on small squares of buttered toast. Heap the spinach on each square. Place a hard boiled egg on top of each and serve.

SPINACH FOR GARNISHING.

Wash and cook a half peck of spinach as directed in the preceding recipe. Sprinkle with salt while cooking and boil five minutes. Then throw into a pan of cold water. This preserves the color. Drain, press out the water and chop as fine as possible. Put in a saucepan with one tablespoonful of butter, sprinkle over a tablespoonful of flour. Stir five minutes. Add a half teaspoonful of salt and half a pint of stock. Stir until boiling, add a grating of nutmeg. Take from the fire and stir in two tablespoonfuls of extra butter, and serve as a garnish for spiced beef, beef à la mode or fricandeau of veal.

SPINACH WITH CREAM.

Prepare the spinach the same as previously directed, but substitute cream for stock and add one teaspoonful of granulated sugar. Serve in a heated vegetable dish.

PURÉE OF SORREL.

½ peck of sorrel,
1 gill of veal stock,
1 tablespoonful of butter,
Salt and pepper to taste.

Wash the sorrel through several waters, cut off the stems, the leaves only are good. Put a half pint of water and a teaspoonful of salt in a saucepan, throw in the sorrel at the first boil. Boil uncovered ten minutes. Drain and chop very fine. Return to the saucepan, add the butter, stock and a palatable seasoning of salt and pepper. Let boil up once and serve with breaded veal cutlet, or it may be served with fricandeau of veal.

SUMMER SQUASH.

Boil, pare and cut into slices three summer squashes. Remove the seeds and cut the slices into squares; put them in a saucepan, cover with boiling water, add a teaspoonful of salt and boil twenty minutes. Drain carefully, mash, turn into a strainer cloth and squeeze until the squash is perfectly dry. Now put in a saucepan, add a teaspoonful of butter, half a teaspoonful of salt and a dash of pepper. Stir until the squash is very hot, and serve in a heated vegetable dish.

FRIED SQUASH.

Pare and cut three squashes into slices a quarter of an inch thick. Dust with salt and pepper. Dip first in egg, then in bread crumbs. Fry the same as egg-plant.

SUMMER SQUASH WITH MELTED BUTTER.

Peel, cut in halves, and then into eighths, and again into eighths, two summer squashes. Boil in salt water twenty minutes. Drain, and arrange neatly on a dish of toast. Dust with salt and pepper and serve with a tureen of English drawn butter.

STEWED TOMATOES.

Pour boiling water over twelve good-sized tomatoes, with a sharp knife remove the skins and hard stem ends, and cut them in small pieces. Put in a porcelain lined or granite saucepan, stew slowly a half hour, then add one tablespoonful of butter, one teaspoonful of sugar, one teaspoonful of onion juice, and a palatable seasoning of salt and pepper. Stew twenty minutes longer or until the desired thickness. If liked, a slice of onion may be added to the tomatoes when they first go over the fire. Thickening of any sort spoils the flavor of the tomatoes.

BAKED TOMATOES.

Choose six large tomatoes, cut slices off the stem ends and with your finger carefully scoop out the seeds. Mix together a half cup of finely chopped, cold boiled ham, twelve chopped mushrooms, two heaping tablespoonfuls of stale bread crumbs, tablespoonful of chopped parsley, one-half teaspoonful of salt, a dash of pepper, and a tablespoonful of butter.

Fill the tomatoes with this mixture, heaping it in the centre. Sprinkle over the tomatoes with bread crumbs, place them in a baking-pan, baste with melted butter. Bake in a hot oven thirty-five minutes. When done, take them up carefully and serve on a flat dish.

These make a fine garnish for baked calves' heads.

STUFFED TOMATOES.

Choose large, smooth tomatoes, slice off the stem ends and with the fingers scoop out the seeds. Put a cup of stale bread crumbs in a bowl, add a tablespoonful of chopped onion, half teaspoonful of salt, a dash of pepper, and a tablespoonful of melted butter. Fill the tomatoes with this stuffing, heaping it in the centre. Place them in a baking-pan, and bake in a quick oven thirty minutes. Lift them carefully with a cake turner, place on a hot dish and serve.

TOMATO FARCI.

Put one layer of sliced tomatoes in the bottom of a baking-dish, then a layer of bread crumbs, sprinkle with salt and pepper. Then put in another layer of tomatoes, bread crumbs, and so continue until the dish is full, having the last layer crumbs. Put over the top a few bits of butter and bake in a quick oven twenty minutes. Serve in the dish in which baked.

FRIED TOMATOES.

Wash and cut in halves six nice, ripe tomatoes, place them in a baking-pan skin side down. Cut a quarter of a pound of butter into small pieces, place over the tomatoes, dust with salt and pepper, stand in the oven ten minutes. Then place them over a fire and fry slowly; the tomatoes should become tender without turning. When done, lift them carefully with a cake turner and place them on a heated dish. Draw the baking-pan over a quick fire, stir until the butter is brown, add two tablespoonfuls of flour, mix until smooth, add a pint of milk, stir continually until boiling, season with salt and pepper, pour over the tomatoes and serve.

Tomatoes in this way make a nice lunch or tea dish and will take the place of a meat dish.

DREDGED TOMATOES.

Choose smooth, solid tomatoes, the little end ripe. Cut into slices an eighth of an inch thick, dust with salt and pepper. Beat an egg in a saucer, add a tablespoonful of boiling water. Dip each slice in egg, then in bread crumbs. When ready to serve the tomatoes put two or three tablespoonfuls of lard or drippings in a frying-pan, when very hot, cover the bottom with slices of tomatoes, fry brown on both sides. Lift carefully, put on a heated dish and serve at once.

If kept warm any length of time, they lose their crispness and become soft.

BROILED TOMATOES.

Cut the tomatoes into halves but do not peel. Place them on a broiler, dust with salt and pepper, and broil over a clear but very moderate fire skin side down, about twenty minutes until tender. When done, put them on a heated dish, pour over melted butter and serve with slices of crisp toast.

CURRIED TOMATOES.

1 quart of stewed or canned tomatoes,
1 cup of rice,
1 teaspoonful of curry powder,
Salt and pepper to taste.

Wash the rice through several waters. Add the powder and salt to the tomatoes, mix well. Put one layer of tomatoes in the bottom of a baking-dish, then a layer of uncooked rice, and then another layer of tomatoes, rice, and so continue, having the last layer tomatoes. Sprinkle the top with bread crumbs. Place a few bits of butter here and there, and bake in a moderate oven forty-five minutes. Serve in the dish in which they were baked. A layer of okra may also be added, and is a great improvement. This makes a nice accompaniment to roasted fowl.

TOMATOES ON THE HALF-SHELL.

Cut the tomatoes in halves without peeling, place them in a baking-pan. Put a piece of butter on top of each and dust with salt and pepper. Stand the pan in the oven and cook the tomatoes slowly about one hour or until perfectly tender. Have ready squares of toasted bread; put a half of a tomato on each square, pour around them Cream Sauce and serve very hot.

ICED TOMATOES.

Scald and peel small, smooth tomatoes, place them on ice until very cold. Serve whole on cracked ice and with a bowl of French dressing.

TOMATOES STUFFED WITH CELERY.

Scald and peel smooth, round tomatoes, cut the slices off the stem end and scrape out the seeds. Place the tomatoes on ice to get very cold. Cut in small pieces the white part of celery, moisten it with French dressing. Fill the tomatoes, place each tomato on a crisp lettuce leaf and serve as a salad.

PICKLED TOMATOES.

Choose small red or yellow tomatoes, prick them with a pin. Put in glass or stone jars, add a half cup of nasturtium seeds and cover with cold cider vinegar. They will be ready to use in about two weeks, and if kept closely covered will keep all winter.

TOMATO FIGS.

6 pounds of tomatoes.   3 pounds of granulated sugar.

Select tomatoes quite ripe but small and smooth. Scald and remove the skins. Place a layer of tomatoes in a porcelain kettle, strew them thickly with sugar, place them over a very moderate fire, and stew very slowly until the sugar appears to have penetrated the tomatoes. Lift each tomato carefully with a spoon, spread them on dishes and stand them in the hot sun one or two days to dry. Sprinkle several times during the drying with granulated sugar. When perfectly dry pack them in jars with layers of sugar between. Care must be taken not to let the rain or dew fall on them while drying.

TOMATO BUTTER.

20 pounds of ripe tomatoes,
8 pounds of sugar,
Juice of four lemons,
4 pounds of apples,
1 tablespoonful of powdered ginger.

Scald the tomatoes and remove the skins. Put in a porcelain kettle with the apples pared, cored and quartered. Stand over a moderate fire one hour, stirring occasionally to prevent sticking. Then add the sugar, lemon juice, and ginger. Cook slowly and stir continually till reduced to the consistency of marmalade. Put into tumblers, or jars and when cold, tie up with two thicknesses of tissue paper. Moisten the top with water or white of egg and when dry place in a cool dark place to keep.

RIPE TOMATO PRESERVES.

Select a half peck of nice, smooth tomatoes not over-ripe, scald, peel and weigh. To each pound allow one pound of sugar, juice and rind of half a lemon, and a small piece of ginger root cut into thin slices. Put all this in a porcelain kettle and cook gently three hours. The tomatoes should not lose their shape but should be clear and tender. Put them into tumblers or jars and stand away to cool. When cold, tie as directed in the preceding recipe. Yellow tomatoes may be preserved in the same manner.

YELLOW TOMATO MARMALADE.

Scald and skin a half peck of yellow tomatoes, large or small, put them in a porcelain kettle, cook thirty minutes, then add an equal quantity of grated pineapple. Weigh or measure and to each pound allow one pound of granulated sugar. Cook slowly one hour, put into tumblers or jars and when cool tie as directed.

PRESERVED GREEN TOMATOES.

Wash one peck of green tomatoes, cover with boiling water and stand aside thirty minutes. Wipe and cut into slices. Slice also six large, juicy lemons; carefully remove the seeds. Put the tomatoes in a porcelain kettle, add the lemons, six pounds of granulated sugar, an even tablespoonful of ground ginger or small pieces of root ginger sliced, and a half pint of water to prevent burning. Cover the kettle and cook slowly one and a half hours, skimming carefully. Stand aside to cool. When cold, bring again to boiling point and *simmer* gently another hour; then put into small jars or tumblers. When cold tie as directed.

TOMATO MANGOES.

Select smooth soft green tomatoes. Cut from the stem end a piece sufficiently large to allow the removal of the seeds without breaking the tomato. Take out the seeds, stand the tomatoes up in a tub, with each top by the side of its corresponding tomato. Sprinkle a teaspoonful of salt in each tomato, cover with cold water and soak twenty-four hours. Drain by turning them upside down. Cut two large heads of cabbage on a slaw cutter, add to it a teaspoonful of ground cloves, a teaspoonful of ground allspice, four tablespoonfuls of whole mustard, and two tablespoonfuls of salt. Mix, stuff this in the tomatoes, put on the tops, tie them tightly with soft twine. Stand the tomatoes upright in a stone jar, cover with cold vinegar and in one week they are ready for use.

A few stuffed peppers or a few hot peppers mixed with the tomatoes greatly improves their flavor. If the vinegar moulds in one or two weeks, drain off, cover with fresh cold vinegar, add two tablespoonfuls of chopped horseradish, which will prevent moulding.

TOMATO CATSUP, No. 1.

Cut ripe tomatoes into slices, put in a stone jar a layer of tomatoes and a layer of salt. Stand aside three days. Then press through a sieve, spice and vinegar to taste, bottle and seal.

TOMATO CATSUP, No. 2.

Tomatoes for catsup should be gathered in August, as later in the season they lose their freshness, becoming watery and more acid. Catsup made in September rarely keeps perfectly well.

1 bushel of tomatoes,
½ pound of sugar,
1½ ounces of black pepper,
1 ounce of ginger root,
½ a gallon of vinegar,
½ pint of salt,
2 ounces of whole mustard,
½ ounce of cloves,
1½ ounces of allspice.

Use all the spices whole. Put the tomatoes, without peeling, on to boil. Cook gently a half hour. Press through a sieve to remove the seeds and the skins. Add all the spices; return the tomatoes to the kettle and boil down until the catsup reaches the proper consistency. It should be a little too thick, of course, to allow the vinegar. Now add the vinegar, and let stand on the back of the stove slowly cooking another hour. Then add the sugar and salt and about half a teaspoonful of cayenne pepper. Bottle and seal while hot.

ENGLISH TOMATO CATSUP.

1 bushel of ripe tomatoes,
½ pound of sugar,
1 ½ ounces of black pepper,
2 ounces ground mustard,
½ ounce of ground cloves,
½ teaspoonful of powdered asafœtida,
½ gallon of vinegar,
½ pint of salt,
1 ½ ounces allspice,
1 ounce of ground ginger,
½ teaspoonful of cayenne,
1 pint of alcohol.

Put the tomatoes on to boil, cook gently a half hour. Press through a sieve to remove the seeds and skin, return to the kettle and boil down to one and a half gallons. Then add the vinegar and evaporate over the fire to one and three-quarter gallons. Now add the sugar, salt and spices. Stir until thoroughly mixed. Put the asafœtida in a teacup, add two tablespoonfuls of warm water, and stir until thoroughly mixed, then turn it into the kettle and stir *continually* until the catsup comes to a boiling point. Then take from the fire and add the alcohol. Bottle and seal while hot.

This recipe has been in constant use in my own family for years, and has been pronounced, by those who have tried it, perfect.

COLD TOMATO CATSUP.

Peel and chop fine a half peck of ripe tomatoes, drain in a colander. Turn into an earthern vessel, add a half cup of grated horse-radish, a half pint of salt, one cup of black and white mustard-seed mixed, two tablespoonfuls of black pepper, two red peppers, two roots of celery chopped fine, two teaspoonfuls of celery seed, one cup of nasturtiums chopped fine, one cup of brown sugar, two tablespoonfuls of ground cloves, two tablespoonfuls of ground allspice, one teaspoonful of cinnamon, one teaspoonful of ground mace, add one quart of cider vinegar. Mix all well together, bottle and seal. The cold tomato catsup will keep one or two years perfectly sweet, and is a very nice accompaniment to cold meats or boiled salt meats.

GREEN TOMATO PICKLES.

1 peck of green tomatoes,
1 ounce of whole allspice,
1 dozen onions,
1½ ounces of black pepper,
¼ pound of ground mustard,
1 ounce of whole cloves,
1 ounce of mustard-seed.

Slice the tomatoes and onions. Then put a layer of tomatoes in the bottom of a jar, then a layer of onions, then a sprinkling of salt, then tomatoes and so on till all are used. Stand aside over night. Next morning drain off all the liquor. Put them in a porcelain kettle, add the spices, cover with vinegar and *simmer* gently fifteen minutes. Put away in stone or glass jars.

TOMATO HONEY.

Select ripe yellow tomatoes, weigh them, cut them into pieces, and put in a porcelain kettle, and for each pound add the grated yellow rind of one lemon; *simmer* gently for thirty minutes, then drain, and press gently through a cheese cloth. Measure the liquor and return it to the kettle, and for each pint add one pound of granulated sugar and four tablespoonfuls of lemon juice. Boil twenty or thirty minutes until a jelly-like syrup is formed. Put in bottles or tumblers for keeping.

MASHED TURNIPS.

Wash, pare and cut into quarters twelve good-sized turnips. Throw them into a kettle of boiling water and boil until tender, about thirty minutes. When done, drain in a colander, pressing lightly to squeeze out all the water. Mash fine, add a tablespoonful of butter, a teaspoonful of salt and a seasoning of pepper. Serve very hot.

TURNIPS WITH POTATOES.

Proceed as in the foregoing recipe. When mashed, add an equal quantity of hot mashed potatoes. Serve in a heated dish.

TURNIPS WITH CREAM SAUCE.

Pare six nice, crisp turnips and cut them into dice. Put them into a saucepan of boiling water and boil thirty minutes. Drain, turn into a heated dish. Pour over a half pint of Cream Sauce and serve.

Turnips cooked this way make a delightful, delicate vegetable to serve with roast poultry. One would scarcely recognize the coarse, mashed turnips so often seen.

BROWNED TURNIPS.

Pare and cut into slices crosswise six good-sized turnips. Boil twenty minutes, drain in a colander. Put two tablespoonfuls of drippings into a frying-pan; when hot, dust the turnips with sugar, put into the fat, turn carefully until the slices are nicely browned. Serve with duck or goose.

RUTA BAGA.

Ruta bagas may be cooked the same as common white turnips. They are exceedingly nice browned to serve with ducks or geese.

TURNIP TOPS OR SPROUTS.

Wash a quarter of a peck of turnip tops in cold water; throw them into a kettle of boiling water, add a teaspoonful of salt, boil twenty minutes, drain. Turn into a vegetable dish garnished with slices of hard-boiled eggs and serve the same as spinach. In the spring of the year turnips become wilted and are not fit to use. Then use the sprouts. They may also be served as a salad, dressed with French dressing.

CREAM VEGETABLE SOUPS.

ARTICHOKE SOUP.

3 good-sized French artichokes, 1 quart of milk,
3 level tablespoonfuls of flour, 2 tablespoonfuls of butter,
Salt and pepper to taste.

Wash the artichokes, throw them into boiling water, boil forty-five minutes, take from the fire, drain, then pull them to pieces and press them through a purée sieve. Put the milk on to cook in a double boiler, add the artichoke to it. Rub the butter and flour together, stir into the hot milk, stirring continually until the milk thickens. Add the salt and pepper, cook ten minutes and serve with tiny chicken forcemeat balls floating in it.

CHICKEN FORCEMEAT BALLS:—Take four tablespoonfuls of chopped, uncooked chicken, add to it an equal amount of stale bread crumbs. Add the white of one egg and a palatable seasoning of salt and pepper. Make this mixture into tiny balls, dropping each, as soon as made, into a kettle of boiling water. *Simmer* gently ten minutes. Lift with a skimmer and place in a soup tureen.

SOUP OF PALESTINE.

6 Jerusalem artichokes,   1 quart of milk,
1 large tablespoonful of butter,   2 even tablespoonfuls of flour,
Salt and pepper to taste.

Scrape and slice six good-sized Jerusalem artichokes, throw them into cold water as soon as sliced. Put them in a saucepan of boiling water and cook one hour. Press through a purée sieve. Put the milk on to heat in a double boiler, add the artichokes. Rub the butter and flour together. Stir it into the hot mixture and stir continually until it thickens. Add the salt and pepper and serve with squares of toasted bread.

ASPARAGUS SOUP.

1 bundle of asparagus,   1 quart of milk,
3 even tablespoonfuls of flour,   1 tablespoonful of butter,
Salt and pepper to taste.

Wash the asparagus, throw it into a saucepan of boiling salted water, boil gently thirty minutes. Take from the water, cut off the tops and put them into a soup tureen. Put the milk on to heat in a double boiler. Press the asparagus through the colander. Rub the butter and flour together, add the milk and stir continually until it thickens. Then add the asparagus that has been pressed through a colander, take at once from the fire, add the salt and pepper and pour over the tops in the tureen.

Canned asparagus may be used for the soup, but must

be handled very carefully or it will curdle the milk. All cream soups must be served as soon as made or they will curdle.

BARLEY SOUP.

| 1 quart of milk, | 2 tablespoonfuls of barley, |
| Yolks of two eggs, | 1 onion, |

Salt and pepper to taste.

Scald the barley, drain, put it into a pint of water. Add the onion and parsley, and if you have three or four small beef bones, add them. *Simmer* gently three hours. Put the milk on in a double boiler, add the barley and the water in which it was boiled, also the onion, which will be soft and tender. Season with salt and pepper. Beat the yolks lightly, put them into the soup tureen and pour in the soup slowly, stirring all the time.

LIMA BEAN SOUP.

1 pint of freshly shelled lima beans,	3 tablespoonfuls of flour,
	1 stalk of celery,
1 sprig of parsley,	1 clove,
1 tablespoonful of butter,	Piece of green pepper,
	1 small onion.

Put the beans in one quart of water, add the parsley, celery, onion, clove, and pepper, and boil three-quarters of an hour. Press through a colander, saving all the liquor in which the beans were boiled. Return this to the kettle. Rub together the butter and flour, stir this into the beans, add one pint of milk and press the whole again through the purée sieve. Put into the farina boiler, season with salt and pepper, bring to boiling point and serve with croûtons.

CROÛTONS:—Butter lightly slices of bread, then cut into dice, rejecting all the crusts. Put the dice in a baking-pan and stand in a moderate oven until the bread is thoroughly dry and golden brown.

CELERY SOUP.

3 roots of celery,
1 tablespoonful of butter,
1 pint of water,
Salt and pepper to taste.

1 quart of milk,
3 even tablespoonfuls of flour,
Piece of onion the size of a silver quarter.

Wash the celery and cut it into small pieces, using all the tops and the root. Cover with a pint of water, boil thirty minutes. Press through a colander. Put the milk on in a double boiler. Add the water and celery, pressed through the colander, also the onion, and if you like, one bay-leaf. Rub the butter and flour together, stir into the hot soup, and stir continually until it thickens. Add the salt and pepper and serve at once. Remove the onion.

CORN SOUP.

1 pint of pressed corn,
2 even tablespoonfuls of flour,
Yolks of two eggs.

1 quart of milk,
1 tablespoonful of butter,

Put the milk on to boil in a double boiler, add the corn cobs from which the corn has been removed. Cover and cook slowly a half hour. Remove the cobs, add the corn, cook twenty minutes more and press through a purée sieve. Rub the butter and flour together, add to the soup and stir continually until it thickens. Beat the yolks of the eggs, put them in the tureen, add gradually the hot soup, season and serve.

PEA SOUP.

Shell a half peck of green peas. Wash the peas, put them in a soup-kettle, cover with cold water, boil twenty minutes. Take out one cup and press the remainder through the purée sieve. Return the soup to the kettle and add one quart of milk and the cup of peas. Rub two ounces of butter and four tablespoonfuls of flour until smooth, stir into the soup, and stir continually until the soup is thick and smooth. It should be the consistency of thick cream. Season with salt and pepper and serve.

PEA SOUP FROM CANNED PEAS.

Press a pint can of peas through a purée sieve. Put one quart of milk in a farina boiler and when hot, add the peas pressed through the sieve. Rub one tablespoonful of butter and two even tablespoonfuls of flour together, add to the boiling soup. Stir until it thickens. Add a half teaspoonful of onion juice, and a palatable seasoning of salt and pepper. Serve immediately.

POTATO SOUP.

4 good-sized potatoes,	1 quart of milk,
Piece of onion the size of a silver quarter,	A sprig of parsley,
	1 tablespoonful of butter,
A stalk of celery or a half teaspoonful of celery seed,	1 bay-leaf,
	2 even tablespoonfuls of flour,
Salt and pepper to taste.	

Put the potatoes on to boil in a quart of cold water. When half done, drain, throw the water away and cover the potatoes with a pint of fresh boiling water. Add the bay-leaf, onion, parsley, and celery and boil slowly until the potatoes are done. Put the milk on to heat in a double boiler. Rub the butter and flour together, add to the hot milk, and stir till it thickens. When the potatoes are tender press them through a purée sieve with the water in which they were boiled. Add the thickened milk gradually to this, return to the farina boiler and when very hot, serve immediately.

This soup cannot stand and is not good warmed up.

RICE SOUP.

½ cup of rice,
2 tablespoonfuls of butter,
Stalk of celery,
1 quart of milk,
½ a small onion,
1 bay-leaf,
Salt and pepper to taste.

Put the milk in a double boiler, add the rice to it. Cook slowly thirty minutes. Keep the boiler covered or the milk evaporates, and you must have at least one quart when the rice is tender. Cut the onion into slices, put with the butter in the frying-pan, cook slowly until the onion is tender but not brown. Then add the celery to the onion and turn the whole into the farina boiler. Add the bay-leaf, cover, and let stand on the back part of the stove fifteen minutes. Then press the whole through a purée sieve, return to the boiler, season with salt and pepper and it is ready to serve.

If the milk evaporates during the cooking and the soup is too thick, add sufficient milk to make it the proper consistency.

SALSIFY OR OYSTER PLANT SOUP.

1 bunch or one dozen salsify roots,
3 even tablespoonfuls of flour,
1 quart of milk,
1 tablespoonful of butter,
Salt and pepper to taste.

Scrape the salsify, cut it into slices, cover with a pint of boiling water, boil slowly one hour. Add to this the milk; do not drain off the water. Rub the butter and flour together, stir into the soup and stir continually until it boils. Add six whole allspice and a blade of mace. Let it stand on the back of the stove ten minutes. Season and serve.

MOCK BISQUE SOUP.

1 quart of milk,
A large tablespoonful of butter,
1 bay-leaf,
A blade of mace,
¼ teaspoonful of baking soda,

1 pint of canned tomatoes or one pint of stewed tomatoes,
A sprig of parsley,
1 teaspoonful of sugar,
3 tablespoonfuls of flour.

Put the tomatoes in a saucepan with the bay-leaf, parsley and mace. Cover and stand on the back part of the stove fifteen minutes. Put the milk in a double boiler; rub the butter and flour together, add to the milk and stir until it thickens. Press the tomatoes through a sieve sufficiently fine to remove the seeds. Then put them into the soup tureen. Add the sugar and soda and then pour in quickly the boiling milk. Stir and serve immediately. This mock bisque soup must not go over the fire after the milk and tomatoes are mixed or they will separate. If not ready to serve, keep the tomatoes hot and the milk hot, but separately. Then mix and add the soda and sugar just the moment of serving time.

PURÉE OF VEGETABLE SOUP.

1 onion,
2 potatoes,
2 tablespoonfuls of rice,
2 tablespoonfuls of corn starch,
1 quart of water,

1 carrot,
1 tomato,
2 tablespoonfuls of butter,
1 pint of milk,
Salt and pepper to taste.

Peel the potatoes and onion and cut them in slices. Put the butter in a frying-pan, add the onion, fry until it is a golden brown. Turn into the soup kettle; add the potatoes, rice, and carrot scraped and cut into slices, add the water, cook slowly until the vegetables are tender, about one hour. Press all through a purée sieve and return to the kettle. Moisten the corn starch with a little cold milk, add to the purée and then add the milk. Stir continually until boiling, season and serve with croûtons.

SOUP CRÉCY.

4 good-sized carrots,	1 pint of water,
1 pint of milk,	Piece of bacon rind or a small
1 onion,	piece of bacon,
2 bay-leaves,	Salt and pepper to taste.

Scrape and grate the carrots into the water; add the bacon, onion and bay-leaves. *Simmer* gently thirty minutes. Then remove the bay-leaves and bacon, add the milk and seasoning and, when boiling hot, serve.

ENGLISH PEA PORRIDGE.

1 pint of split peas,	2 onions,
Stalk of celery,	2 ounces of bread,
3 quarts of water,	1 pint of potatoes,
6 leeks,	2 tablespoonfuls of butter.

Cut the onions into slices. Cut the celery into pieces. Put them with butter in a frying-pan, stir until a golden brown. Then put in the soup kettle with all the other ingredients, cook slowly one hour, skimming at the first boil. If the peas are not tender at the end of this time, boil a little longer till they can be easily pressed through a sieve. Press all through a purée sieve, return to the kettle, and when boiling, season and serve.

This porridge should be quite thick, and if it has the slightest inclination to settle, rub a tablespoonful of butter and two of flour to a smooth paste, stir into the hot porridge till it boils. Serve.

VEGETABLE SOUP WITHOUT MEAT.

1 carrot,	1 root of celery,
1 sweet potato,	1 tablespoonful of butter,
1 turnip,	2 tablespoonfuls of rice,
1 parsnip,	2 quarts of cold water,
1 white potato,	1 bay-leaf,
1 onion,	1 teaspoonful of salt,

1 sprig of parsley.

Cut the vegetables into dice. Put the butter into a frying-pan; and when hot put in all the vegetables but the white potato and fry until a light brown. Then turn the whole, butter and all, into a soup kettle, add the water, rice, bay-leaf, salt, parsley and celery. Let them boil slowly one and a quarter hours. Then add the white potato; boil fifteen minutes longer, season to taste and serve.

VEGETABLE SOUPS WITH MEAT.

DRIED BEAN SOUP.

1 pint of white soup beans,	¼ pound of bacon,
1 soup bone,	1 onion,
2 bay-leaves,	Salt and pepper to taste.

Cover the beans with cold water, soak over night. In the morning drain, put them in a soup kettle with the bacon and small soup bone. Bones left from roast beef will answer. Add two quarts of water and *simmer* gently until the beans are tender, about one and a half hours. Then press through a purée sieve and return the contents to the kettle. Add sufficient water to make it the consistency of cream, bring it to boiling point, season and serve with croûtons.

BLACK BEAN SOUP.

1 pint of black turtle beans,
1 quart of stock or one pound of lean beef,
1 lemon,
1½ quarts of boiling water,
2 hard-boiled eggs,
Salt and pepper to taste,
If wine is used, one gill.

Wash the beans well in cold water, soak over night. In the morning drain, put in a soup kettle with boiling water, if you use beef add it. Cover and *simmer* gently two hours. Now add another pint of boiling water, press all through a purée sieve. Wash the kettle, return the soup to it. Bring it to boiling point, salt and pepper. This soup should be thick, but if too thick, add sufficient water to make it of a proper consistency. Add one tablespoonful of grated onion and pour into the soup tureen over the eggs hard boiled and cut in slices, and the lemon cut in slices. Add the wine and serve at once.

A very good way is to have the eggs hard boiled and cut in slices, and the lemon cut into slices and both covered with the wine about fifteen minutes before the soup goes into the tureen.

CLEAR VEGETABLE SOUP.

1 shin,
1 carrot,
1 sweet potato,
1 ear of corn,
1 cup of beans,
5 quarts of cold water,
1 turnip,
1 white potato,
1 cup of peas,
1 tomato,
1 tablespoonful of rice.

Put the shin in a large kettle, cover with water, *simmer* gently three hours. This may be done the day before, if you wish. Then strain, remove every particle of fat from the surface and return to the soup kettle. If you make it the day before, the fat when cold, will float on the surface and can be removed in one solid cake. The soup or stock will be a perfectly clear jelly. In taking it from the bowl be careful to leave all the sediment behind so that you have a perfectly clear soup. Cut the vegetables into pieces of uniform size and add those requiring the longest cooking first. If you do not, the softer ones will impair the transparency of the soup. The carrot, turnip, sweet potato, beans, and rice may be added one hour before serving. The potato, peas, corn and tomato add twenty minutes before. Season with salt and pepper and serve.

JULIENNE SOUP.

2 quarts of stock,	2 carrots,
1 turnip,	White part of head of celery,
2 onions or six young leeks,	A few pieces of cauliflower,
A head of lettuce,	2 tablespoonfuls of peas,

A few heads of asparagus.

Make your stock according to the preceding recipe. Remove the fat. Put the stock in a soup kettle. Cut the carrot into fancy shapes or strips with a vegetable cutter, cut the turnip in the same way. Cut the onion into tiny pieces and the celery in pieces about half an inch long. Divide the cauliflower into flowerets. Cover all the vegetables with boiling water and boil fifteen minutes. Drain in a colander, then add to the stock and *simmer* gently one hour. Then add the pieces of asparagus heads and *simmer* ten minutes. Then add the lettuce torn into pieces the size of a half dollar, cook five minutes, season with salt and pepper and serve.

LENTIL SOUP.

1 pint of lentils,	2 quarts of stock,
1 onion,	A sprig of parsley,
A sprig of thyme,	1 bay-leaf,
1 tablespoonful of butter,	Salt and pepper to taste.

Wash the lentils, soak over night, in the morning drain

off the water. Wash, put them in a soup kettle, add the stock and *simmer* gently about one and a half hours. Put the butter in a frying-pan, when melted, add the onion sliced, parsley, thyme, and bay-leaf. Fry until a light brown, add this to the lentils and *simmer* a half hour longer. Press the whole through a purée sieve, return to the kettle, boil up once, add the salt and pepper and serve with squares of toasted bread.

If the soup settles after you pour it into the tureen, your sieve is not sufficiently fine or your soup is not thick enough. By rubbing a tablespoonful of butter and one of flour together and adding it to the soup, you will prevent the settling of the thick part to the bottom.

ONION SOUP.

1 large Spanish or three ordinary onions,
2 tablespoonfuls of butter,
2 quarts of stock,
Salt and pepper to taste.

Peel the onions and cut them into slices. Put the butter in a frying-pan, when hot add the onions. Cover and stand on the back part of the stove until the onions are tender without browning. Then put in the soup kettle with the stock, boil gently thirty minutes, add the salt and pepper. Press through a purée sieve and it is ready to serve.

BISQUE OF TURNIP.

4 good-sized ruta bagas,
1 pound of beef,
1 onion,
1 quart of water,
1 pint of milk,
Salt and pepper to taste.

Put the meat into the soup kettle with the water and the onion, add the turnips, *simmer* gently one hour. Then press through a purée sieve, return to the kettle, add the milk, bring to boiling point. Season and serve. If the soup is too thick, add sufficient milk to make it of the proper consistency. One tablespoonful of butter stirred in just before you turn it into the tureen, improves it.

COCK-A-LEEKIE.

1 chicken, about three pounds,
4 quarts of stock,
3 bunches of leeks,
Salt and pepper to taste.

Wash the leeks, take off part of the heads and roots, cover with boiling water. Let them stand five minutes, cut them in pieces. Draw and truss the fowl; put it in a kettle, add the leeks and stock. If without stock, water will answer. Cover and *simmer* slowly three hours, skimming at the first boil. When ready to serve, take out the chicken, remove the skin and cut the meat into dice. Put it into the tureen. Press the soup through a purée sieve, return to the kettle and bring to boiling point. Season with salt and pepper, pour over the chicken and serve.

This soup is better the second day and will bear warming over several times.

HOTCH-POTCH.

1 pound of lean beef,
The neck of mutton,
2 tablespoonfuls of rice,
1 root of celery,
3 cloves,
3 turnips,
1 knuckle of veal,
2 quarts of water,
1 onion,
1 blade of mace,
1 whole green pepper,
1 carrot,
2 quarts of water.

Cut the beef, veal and mutton in small pieces, put in the kettle with the water. Add the other ingredients, cover and *simmer* gently three hours. Season, add a half pint of green peas, cook ten minutes longer and serve.

SOUP, à la MOUSQUETAIRE.

1 pint of shelled peas,
1 pound of beef or a beef bone,
A handful of sorrel,
1 quart of water.

Put the beef, peas, sorrel, and water in a soup kettle and cook over a slow fire about two hours. At the end of that time remove the beef, put it in a baking-pan, spread with butter, dust with salt and pepper, and put in a quick oven until nice and brown. When done, put in the centre of a meat dish, pour the contents of the kettle around and serve. Add seasoning, of course.

POT au FEU.

4 pounds of round beef,
1 onion,
A head of celery,
1 clove of garlic.
2 carrots,
A bay leaf.

Tie the meat into a nice shape, then put in a soup kettle and cover with boiling water. Let *simmer* gently two hours, skim at the first boil. Then put in the garlic cut in small pieces, the onion, bay-leaf, and the other vegetables pared and cut into neat shapes. *Simmer* one hour longer, then, if you like, add two ounces of vermicelli. Boil ten minutes longer, season, and it is ready to serve. Put the meat in the centre of a large platter, arrange the vegetables neatly around it.

SALADS.

From time immemorial lettuce has occupied the most important place in all the salads. The Greeks served it at the end of their meals, while the Romans, who were apt to imitate them, conceived the idea of it as an appetizer, consequently they served it at the beginning of their dinners, accompanied with eggs. Its mild, sweet flavor was supposed to invite the most rebellious appetite. So highly did they treasure it that in the time of drought large beds of it were moistened with sweet wine, when they could not procure water. In those days, also, endless varieties of salads were made, but their materials were limited compared to what we have at present. Now the skillful and ingenious housekeeper may have a different salad almost every day in the month, and such salads may be wholesome, economical and refreshing.

A simple French dressing with lettuce makes an appropriate salad after a hearty meal. String beans nicely boiled and cut into strips lengthwise, also make a delightful after-dinner salad when served with French dressing. Heavy Mayonnaise dressing is best for chicken, lobster, fish and other meat salads, and seems appropriate for some vegetables, as cauliflower, celery, tomatoes.

Americans, as a rule, do not appreciate an after-dinner salad, but if they once accustomed themselves to it, their dinner forever after would be unfinished without it.

To preserve the crispness and flavor of green vegetables for salads, throw them into ice-cold water, then dry on a soft towel and keep in a cold place until wanted. Lettuce is ruined by soaking it in water, and so are tomatoes. The dressing and vegetables should never be mixed until the moment they are ready to serve. In fact, I like to make the dressing at the table, and have the vegetables brought to me crisp and dry and dress them there. The salad must be served in the coldest of dishes, and when well made and garnished, is certainly the most attractive and wholesome dish on the table. In giving recipes for salads the dressings are the important parts. Oil or not oil is an ever-recurring question. While I cannot understand how a person can dislike the flavor of good olive oil, many do. Exact quantities cannot be given, especially if you consider the great diversity of tastes. Delmonico, it is said, used only one egg as a foundation for one quart of oil, with simply salt and cayenne for seasoning; while another noted cook used three eggs as a foundation for one pint of oil with onion and Tarragon vinegar as a flavoring. In preparing all kinds of salad dressing, a silver or wooden fork should be used, and all the materials should be very, very cold, and the oil as pure and fresh as possible.

FRENCH DRESSING.

1 tablespoonful of vinegar,   A dash of cayenne,
½ teaspoonful of salt,   3 tablespoonfuls of olive oil,
¼ teaspoonful of black pepper.

Put the salt and pepper in a bowl and add gradually the oil. Mix in slowly the vinegar, stirring rapidly all the while. As soon as you have a perfect emulsion, that is, the dressing is well blended (the oil and vinegar), it is ready to use, and should be used at once. Many persons think French dressing is simply a mixture of oil and vinegar, and mix in the most careless way, but it should be just as carefully made as Mayonnaise, so that when you pour it over the lettuce it will have a thick white appearance.

Tarragon vinegar may be used in place of plain vinegar. Onion juice or a little garlic may also be added.

AMERICAN SALAD DRESSING.

Yolks of three hard-boiled eggs,   Yolk of one raw egg,
1 tablespoonful of vinegar,   1 gill of olive oil,
½ teaspoonful of salt,   Dash of cayenne,
¼ teaspoonful of mustard.

Before beginning to mix this dressing I would like to say one word about the mustard. I have told you that well-made salad is an exceedingly wholesome dish,—that does not mean the salad containing mustard. Leave the mustard out and almost any one can eat and digest a salad. It is the mustard which makes it unwholesome, but I am sorry to say, Americans seem to prefer unwholesome food.

Mash the cooked yolks until perfectly smooth, then rub in the raw yolk. Work with an elastic bladed knife at least five minutes. Add the salt and pepper and the oil drop by drop. Stir rapidly and steadily all the while. Then add by degrees the vinegar and it is ready to use.

More oil and vinegar may be added if more dressing is required; it is not necessary to use a greater amount of eggs, but let the oil and vinegar make the quantity.

SALAD DRESSING WITHOUT OIL.

½ pint of milk,
1 ounce of butter,
2 tablespoonfuls of vinegar,
1 salt spoon of pepper,

Yolks of three eggs,
2 even tablespoonfuls of corn-starch,
1 teaspoonful of salt.

Put the milk on to boil. Moisten the corn-starch with a little cold milk, add it to the boiling milk, and stir continually until it forms a perfectly smooth, thick paste. Then hastily stir in the yolks well beaten. Cook one minute, take from the fire, add the salt, pepper, butter and vinegar. Stand until icy cold and it is ready to use.

CREAM SALAD DRESSING.

Yolks of three hard-boiled eggs,
Yolk of one raw egg,
2 tablespoonfuls of vinegar,

1 tablespoonful of melted butter,
1 gill of *thick* cream,
½ teaspoonful of salt,
¼ teaspoonful of pepper.

Mash the hard-boiled yolks until perfectly fine and

work in gradually the raw yolk. This must be a perfectly smooth paste. Then add the salt, pepper and melted butter. When well blended add by degrees the cream, working and stirring all the while. Then add gradually the vinegar and it is ready to use. Put in a cold place.

POTATO SALAD DRESSING.

Press one boiled potato through a fine sieve. Add to it while warm, one tablespoonful of butter, and if liked, one tablespoonful of oil. Add one teaspoonful of salt and a dash of cayenne, and work in gradually the uncooked yolks of two eggs. Two hard-boiled yolks should now be added, but first press them through a fine sieve. Add gradually one tablespoonful of either plain or Tarragon vinegar. Add a half teaspoonful of onion juice, or the dish may be rubbed with a piece of onion before putting in the ingredients. When well blended put in a cold place until wanted.

MRS. RORER'S SALAD DRESSING.

1 teaspoonful of onion juice,	1 salt-spoonful of ginny pepper,
1 salt-spoonful of salt,	½ salt-spoonful of white pepper,
4 tablespoonfuls of oil,	½ tablespoonful of Tarragon vinegar.

Put the onion, pepper, salt and ginny pepper in a bowl, add gradually the oil, rubbing until it dissolves. Then work in gradually the vinegar. When you have a thick, well-blended dressing, pour it at once over lettuce or cold boiled string beans and serve.

This is also nice with celery stuffed into tomatoes.

MAYONNAISE DRESSING.

Put the uncooked yolks of two eggs into a clean, cold soup-dish, beat them well with a silver or wooden fork about one minute; then add a half teaspoonful of salt, a dash of cayenne, and, if you like it, a half-teaspoonful of mustard. Work these well together, and then add, drop by drop, a half pint or more of olive oil. You must stir rapidly and steadily while adding the oil. Do not reverse the motion, or it may curdle. After adding one gill of oil, alternate occasionally with a few drops of lemon juice or vinegar. The more oil you use, the thicker the dressing. If too thick, add a half-tablespoonful or more of vinegar, until the proper consistency. More or less oil may be added, according to the quantity of dressing wanted. With care a quart bottle of oil may be stirred into the yolks of two eggs, alternating with a few drops of lemon juice or vinegar, after adding the first gill of oil. It is easier, however, to start with three yolks when making a quart of dressing. In case the dressing should curdle, *i. e.*, the egg and oil separate, which makes the dressing liquid, begin anew at once with the yolks of two eggs in another plate, and after stirring them well, add by teaspoonfuls the curdled Mayonnaise, stirring all the while, and then finish by adding more oil as directed.

In warm weather, it will take only one-half the time, if you put the dish in which you make the Mayonnaise on a piece of ice, or in a pan of ice-water; the oil and eggs should also be cold.

This dressing, if covered closely in a jar or tumbler, will keep in a cool place for one week.

CHICKEN SALAD.

Draw and singe a fowl, put in a kettle with just enough boiling water to keep it from burning, add a slice of onion, a bay-leaf, a few cloves, and a blade of mace. Cover the kettle and cook the chicken slowly until perfectly tender. This method of cooking will make the dark meat almost as white as the white meat. For special occasions use the white meat only; the dark meat can be used for croquettes or other chicken entrées. When done put the chicken away until perfectly cold; it is best always to cook it the day before using. Then remove the skin and cut the meat into dice. Cut and not tear; remove the meat from the carcass in as large pieces as possible. Cut with a sharp knife, laying the meat in blocks a little larger than ordinary dice. Under no circumstances chop it. After it is properly cut, stand away in a cold place until wanted.

Wash, brush and cut the white part of celery into pieces a half inch long. Dry on a soft towel and stand away in the cold until wanted. Now make your Mayonnaise dressing according to the recipe given. To each pint of chicken allow two-thirds of a pint of celery and one cup of Mayonnaise dressing. When ready to serve mix the celery and chicken and dust lightly with salt, white pepper or cayenne; then mix with them the Mayonnaise. Garnish the salad bowl with crisp lettuce leaves, heap in the salad and serve at once. The bowl may also be garnished with the white, crisp celery tops. One cup of whipped cream may be stirred into the Mayonnaise just before putting it over the chicken. This makes a lighter dressing and removes a little of the oily flavor.

The liquor in which the chicken was boiled may be saved for soup.

VEAL SALAD.

This may be made precisely the same as chicken salad, using cold boiled veal instead of chicken.

SWEET-BREAD SALAD.

Clean and parboil one pair of sweet-breads. Then throw them into cold water to blanch a half hour. Remove the fat and every particle of the thin skin. Then cut into thin slices with a silver knife and stand away in a cold place until wanted. When ready to serve put one good-sized slice of onion in the bottom of the salad bowl and arrange over and around it crisp lettuce leaves. On top of this arrange the sweet-breads, cover with Mayonnaise dressing, and serve.

This slice of onion gives just the faintest suspicion of onion and is a great improvement.

CRAB SALAD.

One dozen crabs,
2 roots of celery,
2 heads of lettuce,
½ pint of Mayonnaise.

Boil the crabs in salted water thirty minutes; when perfectly cold, pick out the meat and stand away until wanted. Brush and cut the celery into pieces a half inch long, when ready to serve mix with the crab meat, arrange neatly on a bowl with the lettuce leaves and serve the Mayonnaise in a separate bowl. A very pretty way is to arrange the celery and crab meat in the back shells of the crabs. Stand each on a salad plate on a bed of lettuce leaves, and pass Mayonnaise with them.

LOBSTER SALAD.

This may be made the same, although it is generally served on lettuce leaves without the celery, as it is in season when celery is not.

Boiled fish left over from one meal, may be made into a salad for another. Simply serve on crisp lettuce leaves with Mayonnaise dressing.

Canned salmon may also be served the same way.

SHAD ROE SALAD.

Wash one set of shad roes, put them in a saucepan, cover with boiling water, add a teaspoonful of salt, cover the saucepan and *simmer* gently twenty minutes. Be careful not to boil or the skin will burst. When done, lift from the water carefully with a skimmer and stand aside until perfectly cold. When ready to serve, remove the outside skin, and with a silver knife cut the roe into thin slices. Put a slice of onion in the centre of a dish and arrange around it crisp lettuce leaves. Heap the shad roe in the centre and pass it with a bowl of Mayonnaise dressing.

Shrimps, sardines, and anchovies may also be served on lettuce leaves with Mayonnaise.

ASPARAGUS SALAD.

1 bundle of boiled asparagus,   The rule for French dressing.

Arrange the asparagus neatly on a flat dish, pour over it the French dressing and serve.

This is an exceedingly nice salad for lunch.

FRENCH ARTICHOKE SALAD.

Boil the artichokes until tender, and put them away until perfectly cold. At serving time put one drop of onion juice in the centre of each, arrange neatly on lettuce leaves and pass with them a bowl of Mayonnaise.

BEET SALAD.

Slice and cut into dice sufficient cold beets to make one pint. When ready to serve heap in the centre of the salad dish, and cover with a half pint of sauce tartar. Garnish with curly parsley and serve.

SALAD OF STRING BEANS.

Trim one pint of young beans and boil until tender, when done, drain, and throw into cold water until perfectly cold. Then dry on a soft towel and cut each bean into four pieces lengthwise. Arrange neatly on a salad dish, pour over French dressing and serve.

CAULIFLOWER SALAD.

1 medium-sized head of cauliflower,   Half a pint of Mayonnaise.

Boil the cauliflower as directed for the vegetable, throw into cold water and when perfectly cold, pick apart into little flowerets. Place it on a soft dry towel or napkin. When ready to serve arrange neatly in a salad bowl, cover with Mayonnaise, dust with chopped parsley or chopped chives, and serve.

CABBAGE SALAD.

Cut into shreds the centre of a perfectly white, hard head of cabbage, arrange neatly in a salad bowl, cover with Mayonnaise and serve.

CELERY SALAD.

Cut the white stalks of celery into half inch pieces. To each pint of this allow a little over a gill of Mayonnaise. Dust the celery lightly with salt and pepper, mix with the dressing, heap on a cold dish. Garnish with the white tops of the celery and serve immediately. This salad is decidedly better mixed at the table.

CUCUMBER SALAD.

2 young cucumbers,
1 tablespoonful of vinegar,
4 tablespoonfuls of oil,
½ teaspoonful of salt,
¼ teaspoonful of pepper.

Pare and slice the cucumbers very thin, throw them into cold water one hour, drain and dry. Do not, on any consideration, add salt to the water in which they are soaked. When ready to serve put them in a salad bowl, sprinkle with salt and pepper. Mix well the oil and vinegar, pour them over and serve at once.

Sliced cucumbers should always accompany the fish course.

SALAD OF CUCUMBER AND TOMATO.

Pare and slice two good-sized cucumbers and soak in cold water one hour. Drain on a soft towel. Pare and cut into thick slices two red, solid tomatoes. Cover the bottom of a flat dish with crisp lettuce leaves, arrange the cucumbers and tomatoes alternately in the dish. Serve with French dressing in a boat.

Mrs. Rorer's salad dressing is especially nice with this salad.

EGG SALAD.

Boil six eggs fifteen minutes, when done throw into cold water and remove the shells. Then cut them in slices, arrange them on a bed of lettuce leaves so that one slice overlaps the other. Make a plain French dressing, add to it a tablespoonful of chopped chives and a tablespoonful of chopped parsley. Pour this over the salad, garnish with curly parsley and serve at once.

ITALIAN SALAD.

Cut one carrot or one turnip into slices and then into diamonds, squares, or fancy shapes with a vegetable cutter. Throw them in boiling stock and cook until tender. Have ready two cold boiled potatoes, and if convenient, one beet. Cut in the same way. Then mix all the vegetables carefully in a basin, sprinkle over a tablespoonful of chopped onion or leek, cover with French dressing and serve garnished with water-cress.

In Italy, this is served in a sort of bread crust, called Crôustade.

GERMAN SALAD.

Throw a pint of sauerkraut into boiling water five minutes. Drain, wash well in cold water. Cut into shreds sufficient red cabbage to make one pint, mix this with the sauerkraut. Chop one good-sized onion very fine, add to this a tablespoonful of chopped Chervil, one tablespoonful of grated horse-radish. Arrange endive neatly in a salad bowl, put this mixture in the centre, cover with French dressing and serve.

Despite the homely things that this salad contains it is delicious.

SWEDISH SALAD.

Wash, trim and soak in cold water for one hour a good-sized mackerel, then cover it with boiling water, and *simmer* twenty minutes. Drain and cut into dice. Cut into small blocks sufficient cold roast beef to make a pint. Cut two boiled potatoes into dice. Mix one tablespoonful of capers, one tablespoonful of chopped gherkins, the same of chopped onion, the same of chopped parsley, ten good-sized olives, stoned, and two hard-boiled eggs, chopped fine; add to this the beef, potato and mackerel. Mix carefully, and pour over it a half-pint of French salad dressing; season highly with salt and cayenne. Put the whole in a salad bowl, and lay over the top two dozen cold raw oysters.

CARDINAL SALAD.

Wash and dry two heads of lettuce and a bunch of water-cress; cut two boiled red beets into thin slices; cut a half-dozen small red radishes into slices; chop six hard-boiled eggs rather fine. Arrange the lettuce leaves nicely in a salad bowl; mix the cress, radishes, beets, eggs and one sliced cucumber together, and mix with the whole a half-pint of cardinal Mayonnaise, which is made by adding beet juice to plain Mayonnaise. Put in the salad bowl on the lettuce leaves, and serve at once.

LETTUCE SALAD.

Choose the crisp, centre leaves of a head of lettuce; do not wash unless it is necessary. If, however, obliged to do so, do not break or separate the leaves from the head. Put it in a wire basket, and plunge in and out of a pan of cold water. Shake and dry each leaf carefully on a soft towel. Arrange neatly on a salad bowl and send with it to table a bowl of French dressing.

While it is customary in this country to serve Mayonnaise with lettuce, it is certainly a mistake. The simple French dressing is more appropriate and refreshing.

The following may be arranged and served the same:—

Endive,	Water-cress,	Nasturtium blossom,
Sorrel,	Pepper grass,	Turnip tops,
	Dandelions,	Corn-salad.

SUMMER SALAD.

Peel and slice very thin two good-sized cucumbers. Trim and boil six artichokes. Prepare one root of celery by washing and cutting into small pieces. Slice one bunch or ten small red radishes. Mix the whole. Put them in a salad bowl, sprinkle with chopped Chervil; cover with French dressing and serve.

MACÉDOINE SALAD.

1 boiled beet,
1 dozen boiled string beans,
½ cup of boiled asparagus tops,
1 small onion,
2 tablespoonfuls of cooked green peas,
1 boiled carrot,
A root of celery,
½ pint of Mayonnaise dressing.

All the vegetables should be cut into proper sized pieces and mixed carefully together. They must also be perfectly free from moisture. Arrange neatly in a salad bowl, cover with Mayonnaise dressing and serve.

Lemon juice may be added. Vegetables can be purchased in bottles ready prepared for this salad.

POTATO SALAD.

3 good-sized potatoes,
1 salt-spoon of pepper,
3 tablespoonfuls of vinegar,
1 teaspoonful of salt,
9 tablespoonfuls of olive oil,
1 good-sized onion,
4 sprigs of parsley.

Pare and boil the potatoes, and while boiling prepare the dressing. Put the salt and pepper in a bowl, add gradually the oil, then the vinegar, stir until you have a perfect emulsion. Slice the onion very, very fine, and as soon as your potatoes are done (not soft) remove the skins and cut them into slices. Cut them in the same bowl with the onions. Pour over while hot the dressing, and turn upside down carefully with a fork without breaking the potatoes. Dish, sprinkle over the parsley chopped fine, and stand in a cold place for one or two hours. Garnish the dish with parsley and pickled beets cut into fancy shapes.

Sardines may also be used as a garnish, and for variety, a teaspoonful of anchovy paste may be added to the dressing. It is a great improvement.

MAYONNAISE TOMATO SALAD.

6 small solid tomatoes,
½ cup of Mayonnaise,
Crisp part of one head of lettuce.

Peel the tomatoes without scalding and stand in a cold place till very, very cold. Make the Mayonnaise and stand away until wanted. When ready to serve cut the tomatoes in halves, or if small, simply remove the stem ends. Make a little nest of two or three lettuce leaves, arrange uniformly on a dish, place a half tomato in each nest. Put a tablespoonful of Mayonnaise on top and serve immediately.

TOMATO AND CELERY SALAD.

Peel six good-sized tomatoes. Cut off the stem end and carefully take out the seeds without breaking the tomato. Cut the white part of two stalks of celery into small pieces. Mix two tablespoonfuls of chopped parsley, with the rule for Rorer dressing add it to the celery. Fill this into the tomatoes, stand them on a bed of crisp lettuce leaves and serve at once.

Water-cress may be substituted for celery.

SOUR ORANGE SALAD.

This salad is especially nice to serve with roasted wild duck or woodcock. Peel and cut in slices four sour oranges, arrange on lettuce leaves, cover with Mayonnaise dressing and serve.

ONION SALAD.

Peel and cut in slices two large full green onions. Throw them in cold water twenty minutes. Peel and cut in slices two cucumbers, throw into the same water, drain and dry on a soft towel. Arrange them neatly, slices of cucumber, and onion overlapping. Pour over French dressing and serve.

EGYPTIAN SALAD.

Wash the crisp parts of three heads of endive. Dry on a soft towel and arrange neatly on a flat dish. Sprinkle it with three tablespoonfuls of olive oil, then a tablespoonful of chopped onion. Mix together one tablespoonful of honey (if you have it), if not, one tablespoonful of sugar and one of vinegar. Add a half teaspoonful of salt and a dash of white pepper. Pour over the endive and serve.

CANNING.

Vegetable canning is very much more difficult than fruit canning. Corn and peas are, however, the most difficult vegetables to keep. To be perfectly successful one must choose only perfectly sound vegetables and fruits. If one has to purchase, it is false economy to purchase those on the verge of decay, even at greatly reduced rates, as they will ferment after canning and will then be entirely lost. Besides the loss of the fruits, you frequently lose the cans also. Buy large fruits; after paring they should immediately be thrown into water to prevent discoloration, then boiled in clear water until they are tender, then again in the syrup, and finished as directed in the following recipes.

Small fruits retain their shapes more perfectly if sugared one or two hours before cooking. Large-mouthed glass jars with porcelain-lined or glass tops should be used. They should be properly heated before filling and filled quickly through a wide-mouthed funnel to overflowing. A silver spoon-handle should be passed around the inside of the jars to break any air-bubbles that may be there, then the tops should be screwed on without delay. While filling the jars, place them on a folded towel to prevent breakage. After sealing, stand the jars in a warm part of the kitchen over night. In the morning tighten the covers again, as the glass contracts after cooling. Put them away in a cool (not cold) dry, dark closet. In a week examine each jar carefully, without disturbing it more than is necessary. If the lids are slightly indented, the contents free from any air-bubbles, and the liquid or fruit settled, rest assured your fruit or vegetables will keep. If, on the contrary, you find a frothy appearance around the jars, the lids bulged, and the fruit sharply inclining to the top, open the jars at once to prevent bursting. Fruits may be re-cooked and used at once; never can them again. Vegetables must, of course, be thrown away..

In canning fruits use only the best granulated sugar, and they may be canned with or without sugar, as it takes no part whatever in the preservation of the fruit. Fruit canned with an inferior quality of sugar will become muddled and ferment easily. The surplus juice from the small fruits, such as strawberries, raspberries and plums, may be strained and boiled down for jelly.

A porcelain-lined kettle, rather broad than deep, is best for canning. Copper or brass must be thoroughly cleansed, and even then the articles are more or less imbued with verdigris that is produced by the action of the acids, fruits and vegetables. Small oil or gas stoves are most convenient for canning and preserving, or for jelly making. The kettle being immediately over an even and intense heat, gives the contents a chance to boil quickly, thus retaining the color and flavor of the fruits. If these directions are carefully followed and a small quantity of fruits or vegetables canned at one time, not one can in a hundred will be lost.

FRUITS.—APPLES.

1 pound of sugar,
1 quart of water,
4 pounds of apples,
Juice and rind of one lemon.

Take fine, ripe golden or hollow-cord pippins or bell-flowers. Pare, core and throw them into cold water. When you have sufficient to fill two jars take from the water, weigh, put them in a porcelain-lined kettle, cover with boiling water, bring quickly to boiling point standing over a moderate fire, where they will scarcely bubble until tender enough to admit a straw. While cooking put the sugar in another kettle, stirring with a wooden spoon until the sugar dissolves; add the grated yellow rind and juice of a lemon, boil three minutes. With a perforated skimmer lift the apples from the water, hold them a moment to drain, and slide them carefully into the boiling syrup, continuing this until the bottom of the kettle is nicely covered. Cook the apples in this syrup until they have a clear appearance. Then lift them carefully and slide one at a time into a jar. Fill the jars to overflowing with the syrup, screw on the top and finish as directed.

Quinces may be added to the apples or apples and pine-apples may be mixed. Apples and pine-apple are delicious.

BLACKBERRIES.

To every pound of blackberries allow a quarter of a pound of sugar. Put the berries in a porcelain-lined kettle, sprinkle over the sugar, stand aside one or two hours. Then put over a moderate fire, bring to boiling point, skim and can immediately.

CHERRIES.

Stone the cherries, and if pie or Morello allow a half pound of sugar to every pound of cherries; in ox-hearts, a quarter of a pound of sugar. Proceed as for blackberries. They may also be canned with the stones in, and to my taste are very much better.

All small fruits may be canned after the same fashion.

PLUMS.

Stem and wash the plums, and to every pound of plums allow three-quarters of a pound of sugar. If the plums are large prick the skin to prevent their bursting. If green or yellow gages, it is best to remove the skins by scalding. Cover the fruit with the sugar and stand aside over night. This should be done in large meat plates or earthen dishes. In the morning put sufficient to fill two cans at a time, in a porcelain-lined kettle, bring to a boil, *simmer* until soft without breaking. Skim and can as directed.

PEACHES.

4 pounds of peaches,   1 pound of sugar,
1 quart of water.

Pare the peaches, remove the stones, drop each half at once into cold water to prevent discoloration. Put the sugar and water in a porcelain-lined kettle, stand over the fire and stir continually until the sugar dissolves, boil and skim. Drain the peaches, drop them into the syrup, bring them quickly to the boil and then cook slowly until tender. Lift each piece carefully and arrange neatly in a jar. Then fill the jars quickly to overflowing. Seal and stand aside to cool.

Can pears in precisely the same way.

QUINCES.

Pare, core and quarter the quinces or cut them into rings. Throw them at once into cold water. Save the parings and knotted pieces for jelly, being careful to reject the core and seeds, as they contain mucilage which prevents the liquid jellying. Remember there is a difference between jelly and mucilage. When you pare sufficient to make two jars, take the pieces from the water, put in a porcelain-lined kettle, cover with boiling water and boil until tender. While they are cooking, put the sugar and water in another kettle, allowing half a pound of sugar to half a pint of water for each pound of quinces. Boil and skim. Lift the quinces from the water, put them in the syrup and *simmer* gently. They should scarcely bubble until the quinces are clear and of a bright red color. White quinces may look beautiful, but they are certainly inferior in taste.

If canning several jars of quinces, they should all be boiled in the same water and this water saved to boil with the skins and knotted pieces for jelly. Fresh syrup must, of course, be made for each lot, as you will have only enough to fill the jar.

VEGETABLES.—ASPARAGUS.

Trim the asparagus and throw the pieces into cold water. Then select quart jars. Arrange the asparagus butts down and thoroughly fill the jars. Throw straw or hay in the bottom of a wash boiler, or, better still, White jar holder, stand the jars on this and pour in sufficient cold water to nearly cover. Lay the lids on top, put the boiler over the fire and cover closely. Boil steadily three hours. Take up the jars, see that they are filled to overflowing. This must be done with boiling water. Screw on the covers as tightly as possible, stand aside where the air will not strike them for one or two hours. Then put in a cool place to cool. When cool, again screw on the covers and put in a dark, dry place.

LIMA BEANS.

Select perfectly sound lima beans, put into the jars uncooked, then fill the jars full of cold water. Lay on the tops and finish precisely the same as asparagus, cooking the same length of time.

BEANS.

String the beans, cut them in several pieces, throw them into boiling water, boil rapidly fifteen minutes. Have the jars ready, filled with warm water to slightly heat them. Empty them and fill quickly with the beans, and seal precisely the same as for fruit.

CORN.

Select perfectly fresh corn, remove the husks and silk, and carefully cut the corn from the cob. Corn for canning should never remain in the house over night. It is almost impossible to keep, doing your very best, and will not keep if not freshly picked. Pack the corn in the jars and press down closely, filling each jar to the very top. Put on the tops and screw them down. Arrange in a wash boiler as previously directed. Pour around the jars sufficient cold water, put the lid on the boiler and boil *continuously* three hours. Watch carefully, seeing that there is sufficient water to make a full volume of steam. When done, lift out the jars and screw down the covers as tightly as possible. Stand aside to cool, and when cold give them another screw and keep in a dark, cool place.

CORN AND TOMATOES.

By mixing tomatoes with corn very little difficulty will be found in keeping. While corn ferments quickly alone, the acid of the tomatoes seems to assist in its preservation.

Stew the tomatoes until a proper thickness, then add a sufficient quantity of corn, boil slowly about half an hour. Fill the jars to overflowing, seal as directed.

GUMBO AND TOMATOES.

Gumbo, or okra, and tomatoes may be canned together, and are found very valuable for soups. They also make a delightful scallop for the winter season. Simply cook all together and can as previously directed.

TOMATOES.

Scald the tomatoes and remove the skins. Put them in a porcelain-lined kettle, bring slowly to a boil, *simmer* thirty minutes. Put them boiling hot into the jars, fasten the lids and stand in a cool place. When cold again screw the lids and keep them in a dark, dry closet. Tomatoes are easiest of all vegetables to keep.

PEAS.

Shell freshly gathered peas, wash them and put in the jars uncooked. Fill the jars with cold water and finish precisely the same as lima beans.

CITRON.

Pare off the outer skin, cut the citron in halves, remove the seeds, then divide each half into a number of small pieces. These pieces may be cut into fancy shapes or left plain. Put them in a stone jar, add a half cup of salt to every five pounds of citron. Cover with cold water, stand aside five hours. Drain, cover with fresh, cold water, soak two hours, changing the water three or four times. If you wish them crisp, dissolve one teaspoonful of powdered alum in two quarts of boiling water, add the citron and bring to boiling point. Drain, throw into cold water fifteen minutes and drain again.

Make a syrup from two and a half pounds of granulated sugar, and one and a half quarts of boiling water. Boil and skim. This is to fifteen pounds of fruit. When the syrup is perfectly clear put in the citron and *simmer* until you can pierce it with a straw. Then lift it carefully with a skimmer and spread on large platters. Stand in the hot sun two hours to harden. Chip the yellow rind from one large lemon, add the syrup, then add the strained juice of two lemons, and one and a half ounces of green ginger root cut into thin slices. Boil gently ten minutes and stand aside until wanted.

When the citron hardens, put it, cold, into jars. Bring the syrup again to the boil, strain over the citron. Cover the jars and keep in a dark, dry place.

Watermelon rind may be preserved in precisely the same manner.

RHUBARB JAM.

Wash young rhubarb and cut it into pieces about one inch long. Do not peel. Weigh, and to each pound allow three-quarters of a pound of granulated sugar. Put it in a porcelain kettle, bring slowly to boiling point, then boil and stir continually three-quarters of an hour. Put this in jars and hermetically seal, or it will keep in tumblers tied with paper. This makes excellent pies in winter.

PRESERVED PUMPKIN CHIPS.

Late pumpkins are best for this purpose, and in fact the preserves may be made in winter, as pumpkins will keep perfectly well during the year.

Select a fine ripe one, of a deep yellow color, cut it into halves, then into narrow strips, pare off the outer rind and remove the seeds. Now cut the strips into thin shavings, weigh these shavings, and allow to each one pound one pound of granulated sugar. Secure several dozen of nice, ripe lemons, as it will require one gill of lemon juice to each pound of fruit. Pare the lemons and squeeze out the juice. If you use a glass lemon squeezer it is not necessary to pare them. Spread the pumpkin chips on large platters, sprinkle the sugar over them, then the lemon juice; stand in a cool place over night. In the morning put them into a porcelain-lined kettle, and cook slowly for an hour and a quarter, or until the pumpkin becomes tender, crisp and transparent. Stir carefully and cook slowly, as the pieces must not break or lose their form. Skim frequently as the scum comes to the surface. When the chips are done, lift them carefully with a skimmer, and put them in tumblers or jars; strain the syrup through a flannel bag that has been wrung from boiling water, and pour it over the chips. When cold tie up the same as jelly.

FRUIT JELLIES.

APPLE JELLY.

One recipe for jelly will really answer for all kinds, as the acidity of the fruit has nothing whatever to do with the quantity of the sugar. No matter what kind of jelly, allow one pound of sugar to one pint of juice.

APPLE JELLY.

In apple jelly select the apples with the largest amount of pectin; Lady-blush or fall pippins are best. The first makes a bright red jelly, the latter a jelly almost white. Wipe the fruit, cut into pieces without paring or removing the seeds. Put them in a porcelain kettle and barely cover with water. Cover the kettle and boil about fifteen minutes or until the apples are thoroughly tender. Then drain in a flannel jelly bag. Do not squeeze or press or the jelly will be clouded. To every pint of juice allow one pound of granulated sugar. Put the juice in a porcelain kettle, bring quickly to a boil, add the sugar, stir until the sugar dissolves. Then boil rapidly and continuously until it jellies, about fifteen or twenty minutes.

It may be necessary to boil it thirty or thirty-five minutes before it jellies properly. It is wise, however, to commence testing after the first fifteen minutes' boiling. To do this, take out a teaspoonful of boiling jelly, put it on the bottom of a saucer, and stand in a cold place for a moment. Then scrape to one side with a spoon. If jellied, the surface will be partly solid. If it remains liquid, go on boiling and try again. Remember while that jelly has been cooling, the boiling is going on, and it is wise to try again at once. If boiled past jellying point, you will have a thick, sticky syrup and nothing will make it jelly. This mistake occurs frequently where persons do not understand the chemical process of jelly making; they boil it too long.

Just as soon as the surface in the saucer jellies, roll the tumblers quickly in boiling water; remove the jelly from the fire and fill the tumblers; stand aside uncovered for twenty-four hours. Then fasten the tops with two layers of tissue paper; the edges may be pasted down with the white of egg. Do not use metallic covers or even pasteboard, or your jelly will become sour and ooze out of the tumblers. After the tops are thoroughly fastened and the edges dry, dip a paste-brush or sponge in water and just moisten the top of the paper. This moistening stretches the paper, and as it dries again it shrinks and forms a covering as smooth and tight as bladder skin. I do not recommend jelly covered with brandied paper. In my hands it is never satisfactory. Jelly in cooling forms its own airproof cover, and then, if it has a porous top, like paper, will keep forever. A dark, cool closet is best for it. All jellies can be made after this recipe.

CRAB APPLE JELLY.

Cut the crab apples into halves, then into quarters, weigh, put in a porcelain kettle, and to each five pounds allow one pint of water. Proceed and finish precisely the same as for apple jelly.

BLACKBERRY JELLY.

The uncultivated blackberries are best for jelly ·and should be rather under than over ripe. Put the berries in a stone jar, stand in a kettle of cold water, cover the top of the jar and heat slowly until the berries are soft. Then put a small quantity at a time in a jelly bag and squeeze out all the juice. Measure this juice and allow one pound of granulated sugar to one pint. Turn the juice into a porcelain-lined kettle and bring to boiling point over a brisk fire. Put the sugar in earthen dishes and stand in the oven to heat. Boil the juice rapidly and continuously twenty minutes. By this time the sugar should be very hot, not brown. Turn it in hastily at the end of twenty minutes, stirring until the sugar dissolves. Dip the tumblers quickly in hot water. Watch the liquid carefully and as soon as it goes to boil, take from the fire and fill the tumblers. If you follow this recipe carefully success is sure.

If, on the other hand, you fail, make up your mind it is not the fault of the recipe, as it has been well tried. If the fruit is very ripe, or has been picked a day or longer, your jelly will never be firm, and the longer you boil it the more liquid it will become. In fact, it will become syrup.

Currant, damson and grape jelly may be made in precisely the same manner.

PEACH JELLY.

This should be made the same as apple jelly, and is the hardest of all jellies, except pear, to make.

RHUBARB JELLY.

Wash and wipe the stalks, and, without paring, cut them in pieces an inch long. Put in a porcelain kettle, allowing one pint of water to four pounds of rhubarb. Boil to a soft pulp, turn into a jelly bag and finish precisely the same as apple jelly.

BRANDIED PEACHES.

Take large white or yellow free stone peaches, not over ripe. Scald them by pouring over boiling water, cover and let stand till the water becomes cold. Repeat this scalding, then take them out and rub with a soft cloth until perfectly dry. Put into stone jars; cover with brandy. Tie paper over the tops of the jars and let remain for one or two weeks. Then make the syrup from one pound of granulated sugar, and a half pint of water to each pound of peaches. Boil and skim. Put the peaches in this syrup and *simmer* till tender. Take out, drain and put in glass jars. Stand the syrup aside to cool; when cold, mix equal quantities of syrup and brandy in which you had the peaches. Pour over the peaches, tie up and put away.

If you prefer the peaches pared, simply pare them, cook until tender in the syrup, place them in jars. When the syrup is cold mix with it an equal quantity of brandy, pour this over the peaches, seal, and keep in a cool, dark place.

TO PICKLE LIMA AND STRING BEANS.

Lima beans and string beans may be packed in salt precisely like cucumbers; that is, a layer may be put in the bottom of a cask, then a layer of salt, then another layer of beans. The top of the cask should be fixed precisely the same as for salting cucumbers. In winter, when ready to use, wash thoroughly in cold water and soak over night in clear cold water. Then cook the same as fresh vegetables, changing the water once or twice while cooking. To my taste, this way of preserving beans is far better than canning.

Green tomatoes, sliced, may be prepared in precisely the same manner.

The following is a list of vegetables and their season for pickling:—

Artichokes—July and August.
Beans—July and August.
Cabbage—September.
Red cabbage—September.
Cauliflower—August and September.
Celery—October and November.
Cucumbers—July to the middle of August.
Martynias—July and August.
Musk-melon and cantaloupe—First to the middle of September.
Nasturtiums—August and September.

Onions—August.
Parsley—October.
Peppers—August.
Tomatoes (green)—September.
Tomatoes (ripe)—August.
Walnuts—Latter part of June, or the early part of July, the first week the walnuts form.

SPICED CANTALOUPE.

Cut the cantaloupes in halves, remove the seeds, then cut in thin sections, take off the rind. When you have a sufficient quantity, weigh the pieces and to each seven pounds allow :—

4 pounds of sugar,	1 pint of vinegar,
½ ounce of ginger root,	1 teaspoonful of ground cloves,
2 teaspoonfuls of ground allspice,	2 teaspoonfuls ground cinnamon,

½ teaspoonful of ground mace.

Mix the spices and divide them into four parts; put each part in a small square of muslin, tie tightly, allowing sufficient room for the spices to swell. Put the sugar and vinegar in a porcelain-lined kettle, add the spices, and ginger root, scraped and cut into slices. Stand the kettle over the fire, and when the contents are boiling add the cantaloupe. Take at once from the fire and stand aside in a cool place over night. Next day, drain all the liquor from the cantaloupes and in a porcelain kettle bring it again to the boiling point. Pour this over the cantaloupes and stand aside until the next day. The following morning drain and heat the syrup as before, and do this for nine consecutive days. The last day boil the cantaloupes until perfectly tender, a small quantity at a time. Then the liquor must be boiled down until a thick syrup and just enough to cover the fruit. Put in jars or tumblers and tie up for keeping.

The following fruits must be spiced in precisely the same manner, and if directions are carefully followed success is sure, and the fruit will be perfectly delicious:—

Apples, peaches, cherries, pears, plums, quinces, watermelon.

FLAVORED VINEGARS.

CELERY.

¼ pound of celery seed or a half dozen roots of celery, 1 quart of cider vinegar, 1 teaspoonful of salt, 2 teaspoonfuls of granulated sugar.

If you use the celery seed, simply mix all the ingredients together, put in a porcelain-lined kettle, bring to boiling point. When cold, bottle, shake every day for two weeks, strain through a fine cloth or filter. Bottle and cork tightly. Put away to flavor salad dressings and sauces.

If the celery roots are used, take off the outside and cut the roots into thin slices, add to the vinegar and proceed precisely the same as when you use the celery seed.

CHILI VINEGAR.

This is made by simply infusing fifty small peppers in one pint of best white-wine vinegar.

HORSE-RADISH VINEGAR.

1 teacup of grated horse-radish, 1 quart of cider vinegar, 1 tablespoonful of granulated sugar.

Put the horse-radish in two glass jars, bring the vinegar to the boiling point, add the sugar and pour over the horse-radish. Screw the tops on the jars, shake once a day for one week. Strain, bottle, and seal, and it is ready to use.

ONION VINEGAR.

1 quart of vinegar,
2 teaspoonfuls of granulated sugar,
1 teaspoonful of salt,
2 large onions.

Grate the onions, mix with them the salt and sugar, let stand two hours and add the vinegar. Turn into bottles, shake every day for two weeks, strain through a fine cloth, bottle, cork, and seal.

This onion vinegar may be used for salads and sour meat dishes where a very delicate onion flavor is desired.

TARRAGON VINEGAR.

Put in a wide-mouthed bottle one cup of freshly gathered tarragon leaves. Cover with a quart of good, cold cider vinegar. Cork bottle and stand aside two weeks. Shake frequently. Then strain and squeeze through a flannel bag. Pour into small bottles, cork, seal and keep in a cool place.

This vinegar is an agreeable addition to all salads and fish sauces.

SOUP POWDER.

Take of lemon peel, thyme, sweet marjoram and parsley each one ounce. Dry carefully on paper in a warm oven, then pound in a mortar and rub through a fine sieve. Add one drachm (one teaspoonful) of powdered celery seed, bottle and cork.

One teaspoonful of this may be added to each quart of soup.

HOW TO DRY HERBS.

It is of the utmost importance that food should be well seasoned and palatable. Herbs and seasoning are as important as the food itself. They bring back the languid appetite and encourage one to eat when he would not otherwise do so. During the summer, when herbs are in their highest state of perfection, full of juices and just before flowering, they should be gathered and dried. This should always be done on a perfectly dry day, early in the morning or after sundown. Cleanse thoroughly from dust and dirt, cut off the roots and spread the herbs on squares of brown paper. Put them in a warm oven, dry quickly, to preserve the flavor. If allowed to dry gradually the heat dries off the aroma and they will be almost tasteless. Care must be taken that they do not brown or scorch, as this also destroys the flavor.

When dry, pick the leaves from the stems, put them into bottles or jars and cork tightly. They must be perfectly cold before going into the bottles or they will sweat and sour. Mark each bottle or jar plainly on the outside, to save confusion when wanted for use.

TO SERVE FRUIT.

The French, when serving fruit, exhibit much greater taste than the Americans. The arrangements are not only better, but also the method of serving and the decorations. For instance, strawberries are served whole, without being stemmed, and a small dish of powdered sugar is passed with them, or sometimes they are dipped in fondant, at others, in white of egg and powdered sugar.

Peaches are served in a pretty basket, decorated with fall flowers, and here and there bunches of their own leaves.

Hollyhocks are particularly appropriate. The beautiful white and red currants may be dipped in white of egg, then in sugar and dried on a sieve, then neatly arranged on a pretty glass dish garnished with freshly picked roses. These, as you can readily understand, will make a most beautiful breakfast dish. Cherries should be served in large bunches, and may be mixed with other fruits that are in season at the same time. All fruit should be served cold; some, however, will bear to be chilled, while the flavor of many fruits is entirely destroyed by chilling.

Watermelons and cantaloupes should be first washed, then put in a cold place several hours before serving. To serve them, cut them in halves, cut thin slices from the convex ends, allowing them to stand firmly on a plate. Scoop out the pulp of the watermelons in egg-shaped pieces with a spoon. Cantaloupes should be served in halves, the seeds carefully removed, the fruit eaten with a spoon. The large banana cantaloupes, of course, should be cut in convenient-sized pieces. Sugar, salt and pepper should be passed with them. Cantaloupes are pretty, served on a bed of fresh grape leaves.

Pineapples should be pared with a silver knife, the eyes carefully removed, and the fruit then picked into small pieces with a silver fork; cutting destroys the flavor. Deluge the pieces in sugar and stand away for one or two hours to get perfectly cold.

Raspberries, one of the most delicate of all fruits, should be very carefully looked over and kept in a cool place until serving time. Then serve in a pretty glass dish; they must never be sugared before serving; pass sugar with them. Raspberries may also be moistened with orange or currant juice, just before being sent to the table. Blackberries should be carefully looked over and slightly chilled before serving; they must not, however, be icy cold. They should be sugared about five minutes before serving time and arranged in a pretty glass dish. A very pretty way to serve small fruit is to have heaped in the centre of a large, flat glass dish, a mound of whipped cream with the fruit around it.

TO POP CORN.

Shell perfectly dry pop-corn. Put about half a cupful (one gill) of corn in an ordinary corn popper, a square wire pan with a long handle. Shake it over a clear hot fire until thoroughly dry, and as soon as it begins to pop shake rapidly. If the fire is too hot it will scorch the corn and prevent its popping. The more rapidly you shake, exposing all sides of the corn to the air, the better and more quickly it pops. When the popping ceases open the popper, turn the corn into a large bowl. Have ready about two tablespoonfuls of melted butter; pour this slowly over the corn, stirring constantly with a wooden fork. The corn must be thoroughly greased without being oily. Dust lightly with salt and it is ready to serve. This is the more wholesome way of serving pop-corn. Some prefer it moistened with syrup, and in that case it is more indigestible.

POP-CORN BALLS.

Put a quarter of a pound of sugar and one gill of water in a saucepan. Boil five minutes, skim. This should form a rather thick syrup. Pop the corn as directed, turn into a bowl and pour the syrup in a fine stream over the corn, stirring all the while. A few drops of lemon juice or vanilla may be added to the syrup. Grease your hands lightly, take about two tablespoonfuls of the corn and press gently in the form of a ball. Stand these balls on a greased paper to dry and they are ready to use.

BILLS OF FARE.

It is frequently of great convenience to housekeepers to have arranged for them a few simple, as well as more elaborate bills of fare. The first are intended to act as guides for ordinary family tables, the second as assistants to a company luncheon or dinner. Still, from a proper standpoint, the company luncheon should never be more elegant than the everyday family table. To a well living family, the announcement of one or two guests means only two extra plates at the table.

An appropriate and healthful bill of fare implies both taste and discrimination. For instance, heavy soup should never be served where a large dinner is to follow. A clear, light soup should always precede a course dinner, and a heavy soup a small dinner or lunch. If one wants a more elaborate bill of fare, let raw oysters precede the soup, and this be followed by fish. Potatoes of some kind should be served with fish, also sliced cucumbers. Radishes and gherkins, salted almonds, olives and such dishes as are considered appetizers, should be placed on the table immediately after the soup, and allowed to remain until the table is cleared for dessert. Never serve more than two vegetables with any one course, and do not feel it absolutely necessary always to serve potatoes. Rice is much more appropriate with lamb, mutton or chicken, and for my own taste, I prefer it with veal. In fact, one can serve veal with either spinach or chervil, omitting potatoes entirely. Green peas and asparagus tops accompany lamb; the course should not be spoiled with potatoes. Light entrées, such as sweetbreads, croquettes, meat patties, may follow the fish. Peas may be served at the same time. Black-birds, reed-birds or any small birds may be served with lettuce and French dressing. Small chicken croquettes and lobster cutlets are delightful served this way. With duck, wood-cock, snipe or partridge, serve baked macaroni with cheese. Let the salad be a course by itself, a water cracker and small bit of cheese alone accompanying it.

For breakfast and supper it is not necessary always to have a meat dish, especially during the heated term. The following bills of fare are arranged so that each day contains a luncheon and a supper. This will accommodate persons dining in the middle of the day and also those who dine in the evening.

SPRING BILLS OF FARE.
BREAKFAST.
Sliced Oranges,
Oatmeal, Sugar and Cream

Fried Brook Trout,   Plain Omelet,
Stewed Potatoes,
Rice Waffles,   Coffee.

LUNCH.
Broiled Lamb Chops, Tomato Sauce,
Parker House Rolls,
Mayonnaise of Salmon,

Wafers,   Cheese,
Preserved Ginger,   Wine Biscuit,
Tea.

DINNER.
Cream of Asparagus Soup,

Braised Beef's Tongue,   Potato Puff,
Spinach, Egg Sauce,   Buttered Beets,
Lettuce Salad, French Dressing,
Wafers,   Cheese,
Orange Bavarian Cream,
Coffee.

SUPPER.
Thin Slices of Cold Tongue,   Water-cress,
Milk Biscuit,   Honey,
Gingerbread,   Tea.

SPRING BILLS OF FARE.

BREAKFAST.
Baked Bananas,
Hominy, Sugar and Milk,
Panned Beefsteak, Shirred Eggs,
Plain Muffins, Coffee.

LUNCH.
Fish Cutlets, Cream Sauce,
Sliced Cucumbers, Toasted Cheese,
Stewed Fruit, Wafers,
Tea.

DINNER.
Herb Soup,
Boiled Leg of Mutton, Caper Sauce,
Boiled Rice, Stewed Tomatoes,
Salad of Water-cress,
Wafers, Cheese,
Caramel Pudding,
Coffee.

SUPPER.
Thin Slices of Cold Mutton, Potato Roll,
Preserved Cranberries, Apees,
Russian Tea.

BREAKFAST.
Stewed Rhubarb,
Wheat Granules, Sugar and Cream,
Broiled Ham, Beauregard Eggs,
French Fried Potatoes,
Rice Muffins, Coffee.

LUNCH.
Fried Oysters, Water-cress,
Cold Slaw, Cheese Soufflé,
Lemon Jelly, New York Cookies,
Tea.

DINNER.

Clear Soup with Green Peas,
Roasted Chicken, Giblet Sauce, Cranberry Jelly,
Bermuda Potatoes, Parsley Sauce, Cauliflower,
Asparagus on Toast,
Salad of String Beans,
Wafers, Fairy Toast, Cheese,
Coffee.

SUPPER.

Chicken Salad, Milk Biscuit,
Preserves, Rolled Jelly Cake,
Tea.

BREAKFAST.

Shaddocks,
Moulded Farina, Whipped Cream,
Stewed Kidney, Saratoga Potatoes,
Spanish Omelet,
Pop-overs, Coffee.

LUNCH.

Deviled Clams, Oatmeal Wafers,
Banana Fritters, Powdered Sugar,
Dover Cake, Cocoa.

DINNER.

Purée of Vegetables,
Irish Stew, Boiled Rice.
Sliced Cucumbers,
Oyster Salad,
Wafers, Cheese,
Rhubarb Pie,
Coffee.

SUPPER.

Fricassee of Oysters, Tea Rolls,
Canned Peaches, Water Crackers,
Tea.

SUMMER BILLS OF FARE.

Breakfast.

Cantaloupes,

Oat Flakes,   Whipped Cream,

Broiled Tomatoes, Cream Sauce,
Fried Potatoes,

Toast,   Coffee.

Lunch.

Deviled Crabs,   Brown Bread,

Sliced Tomatoes,

Strawberries and Cream,   Iced Tea.

Dinner.

Julienne Soup,

Panned Spring Chicken,   Cream Sauce,

New Potatoes,

Peas,   Asparagus,

Lettuce Salad,   French Dressing,

Wafers, Cheese,

Strawberry Ice Cream,   Coffee.

Supper.

Lobster—Terrapin Style,   Milk Biscuit,

Fruit,   Cake,

Tea.

Breakfast.

Iced Strawberries,

Wheat Granules,   Sugar and Cream,

Fried Black Bass,   Parsley Omelet,

Stewed Potatoes,

Plain Muffins,   Coffee.

Lunch.

Creamed Sweetbreads,   Stuffed Potatoes,

Thin Bread and Butter,

Sugared Raspberries,   Lemonade.

DINNER.
Sand Clams on the Half Shell.
Spring Lamb, Mint Sauce,
New Potatoes, Peas,
Baked Tomatoes,
Lettuce Salad, French Dressing,
Wafers, Cheese,
Frozen Fruit,
Coffee.

SUPPER.
Sheep's Tongues in Jelly, Water-cress,
Thin Bread and Butter,
Sugared Fruit, Iced Tea.

BREAKFAST.
Iced Currants,
Boiled Rice, Sugar and Cream,
Corn Oysters, Broiled Tomatoes,
Pop-overs, Coffee.

LUNCH.
Mayonnaise of Salmon on Lettuce Leaves,
Brown Bread and Butter,
Sugared Berries,
Lemonade.

DINNER.
Cantaloupes,
Breaded Cutlets, Tomato Sauce,
Peas, String Beans,
Buttered Beets,
Mayonnaise of Cauliflower,
Wafers, Cheese,
Raspberry Water-Ice,
Coffee.

SUPPER.
Clam Fritters, Sliced Tomatoes,
Sugared Fruit, Sponge Fingers,
Tea.

Breakfast.

Blackberry Mush,
Broiled Chicken, Sliced Tomatoes,
Potatoes à la Béchamel,
Rice Muffins, Coffee.

Lunch.

Lobster Cutlets, Cream Sauce,
Sliced Tomatoes,
Cantaloupes,
Lemonade.

Dinner.

Cream of Tomato Soup,
Broiled Steak, Corn,
Stewed Cucumbers, Mashed Potatoes,
Lettuce Salad, French Dressing,
Wafers, Cheese,
Frozen Strawberries,
Coffee.

Supper.

Cold Boiled Ham, Tomato Salad,
Parker House Rolls,
Sugared Fruit, Tea.

AUTUMN BILLS OF FARE.

Breakfast.

Cantaloupes,
Oatmeal, Sugar and Cream,
Broiled Birds, Toast,
Sliced Tomatoes,
Wheat Granule Gems, Coffee.

Lunch.

Welsh Rarebit, Rice Croquettes,
Sliced Cucumbers,
Gingerbread, Cocoa.

DINNER.

Roast Duck,
Boiled Rice,
Wafers,
Purée of Carrots,
New Turnips, Browned,
Mayonnaise of Tomatoes,
Peach Short Cake,
Coffee.
Olive Sauce,
Corn Pudding,
Cheese,

SUPPER.

Stewed Oysters,
Sugared Fruit,
Cold Slaw,
Tea.
Hot Bread,
Berwick Sponge Cake,

BREAKFAST.

Baked Apples,
Moulded Farina,
Fried Perch,
Plain Boiled Potatoes,
Johnny Cake,
Whipped Cream,
Ham Omelet,
Coffee.

LUNCH.

Beef Croquettes,
Sliced Tomatoes,
Sugared Peaches,
Tea.
Peas,

DINNER.

Marrow Ball Soup,
Roasted Shoulder of Veal,
Squash,
Browned Parsnips,
Lettuce Salad,
Wafers,
Ice Cream,
Coffee.
Brown Sauce,
Scalloped Potatoes,
French Dressing,
Cheese,

SUPPER.

Sardines on Toast,
Tomato Salad,
Sugared Fruit,
Tea.
Slices of Lemon,
Marvels,

WINTER BILLS OF FARE.

BREAKFAST.
Stewed Pears,

Oatmeal,   Sugar and Cream,
    Broiled Chops,   Tomato Sauce,
          Saratoga Chips,
Boston Brown Bread,   Coffee.

LUNCH.
Sweetbread Cutlets,   Cream Sauce,
      French Breakfast Rolls,
        Cucumber Salad,
          Cantaloupes.

DINNER.
Bisque of Oyster,

Larded Fillet of Beef,   Mushroom Sauce,
    Potato Croquettes,   Baked Tomatoes,
       Sorrel Salad,   French Dressing,
Wafers,   Cheese.
          Frozen Peaches,
            Coffee.

SUPPER.
Thin Slices of Cold Meat,   Sauce Tartare,
         Potato Salad,
Sugared Fruit,   New England Loaf Cake,
            Tea.

WINTER BILLS OF FARE.

BREAKFAST.
Oranges,

Oatmeal,   Sugar and Cream,
Broiled Salt Mackerel,   Parsley Sauce,
       Stewed Potatoes,   Omelet,
      Fried Indian Mush,   Syrup,
               Coffee.

LUNCH.
Oyster Omelet,   Peas,
       Thin Bread and Butter,
Molasses Wedding Cake,   Cocoa.

DINNER.
Purée of Celery,
Roasted Rib of Beef, Yorkshire Pudding,
Stewed Turnips, Buttered Beets,
Baked Potatoes,
Lettuce Salad, French Dressing,
Wafers, Cheese,
Apple Tart,
Coffee.

SUPPER.
Fried Oysters, Mayonnaise of Cabbage,
Compote of Apples, Sponge Fingers,
Coffee.

BREAKFAST.
Baked Pears,
Wheat Granules, Sugar and Cream,
Broiled Steak, Sauce Bearnaise,
French Fried Potatoes,
Rice Crumpets, Coffee.

LUNCH.
Creamed Fish, Potato Puff,
Chicken Patties,
Preserved Ginger, Wafers,
Russian Tea.

DINNER.
Clear Soup with Croûtons,
Roasted Loin of Pork, Apple Sauce,
Mashed Potatoes, Stewed Cabbage,
Browned Turnips,
Lettuce Salad, French Dressing,
Wafers, Cheese,
Cerealine Blocks with Jelly,
Coffee.

SUPPER.
Ham Croquettes, Tomato Sauce,
Thin Bread and Butter,
Stewed Fruit, Oatmeal Wafers,
Tea.

WINTER BILLS OF FARE.

BREAKFAST.
Stewed Apples,
Oatmeal, Sugar and Cream,
Broiled Sheeps' Kidneys, Bacon,
Rice Omelet,
Johnny Cake, Coffee.

LUNCH.
Beauregard Eggs, Chipped Beef,
Parker House Rolls,
Grapes,
Tea.

DINNER.
Calf's Head Soup,
Roasted Turkey, Giblet Sauce,
Stewed Cranberries,
Oyster Plant Fritters, Baked Potatoes,
Browned Sweet Potatoes,
Mayonnaise of Celery,
Wafers, Cheese,
Plain Plum Pudding,
Coffee.

SUPPER.
Fried Chicken, Cream Gravy,
Waffles,
Canned Peaches, Lady Cake,
Coffee.

BREAKFAST.
Grapes,
Oatmeal, Whipped Cream,
Broiled Ham, Shirred Eggs,
Hashed Potatoes,
Rice Muffins, Coffee.

LUNCH.
Boudins, Cream Sauce,
Stuffed Potatoes,
Hot Gingerbread, Cocoa.

DINNER.
Dried Bean Soup without Meat,
Baked Rock, Egg Sauce,
Cucumber Pickles,
Boiled Potatoes, Peas,
Oyster Plant, Cream Sauce,
Mayonnaise of Cabbage,
Wafers, Cheese,
Orange Bavarian Cream,
Coffee.

SUPPER.
Raw Oysters,
Chicken Salad, Milk Biscuit,
Canned Fruits, Crackers,
Coffee.

WEDDING BREAKFASTS.

SPRING.
Baked Bananas,
Broiled Shad, Roe Sauce,
Parisienne Potatoes,
Breaded Lamb Chops, Tomato Sauce,
French Rolls,
Sweetbread Cutlets, Cream Sauce,
French Peas,
Fricassee of Chicken, Cerealine Blocks,
Muffins, Coffee.

SUMMER.
Melons,
Fried Brook Trout, Sauce Tartare,
Stewed Potatoes,
Broiled Spring Chickens, Cream Gravy,
Peas,
Woodcock, Baked Macaroni,
Mayonnaise of Tomatoes,
Frozen Peaches,
Coffee.

LUNCH.

AUTUMN.

Sugared Peaches,
Fried Oysters, Sauce Tartare,
Olives, Gherkins, Chow Chow,
Broiled Tenderloin of Beef, Mushroom Sauce,
Potato Croquettes,
Reed Birds on Toast, Cranberry Jelly,
Mayonnaise of Cucumbers and Tomatoes,
French Rolls, Coffee.

WINTER.

Bouillon,
Broiled Sardines on Toast, garnished with Water-cress and Slices of Lemon,
Baked Sweetbreads, Peas,
French Rolls,
Venison in Chafing-dish, Currant Jelly,
Baked Macaroni,
Waffles, Honey,
Coffee.

LUNCH.

SPRING.

Raw Oysters on Half Shell,
Bouillon in Cups,
Cusk à la Créme, Potato Puff,
French Rolls,
Sweetbread Patties,
Small Chicken Croquettes, Lettuce Salad
Water Biscuits,
Cheese Ramakins,
Orange Soufflé, frozen,
Fruit,
Coffee.

SUMMER.

Orange Sherbet in Punch Glasses,

Frogs' Legs, French Peas,
Olives, Gherkins, Salted Almonds,

Broiled Spring Chickens, Sauce Tartare,
Potatoes with Cream Sauce,
Tomato Salad Garnished with Radishes and
Nasturtium Blossoms,
Toasted Cheese,
Frozen Strawberries,
Coffee.

AUTUMN.

Bouillon,

Deviled Crabs, Olives, Celery,

Baked Sweetbreads, Tomato Sauce,
Parker House Rolls,

Chicken Croquettes, French Peas,

Shrimp Salad,
Cheese Fingers,
Frozen Peaches,
Coffee.

WINTER.

Raw Oysters on Half Shell,
Bouillon,

Gherkins, Olives, Salted Almonds,
Lobster Cutlets, Cream Sauce,

Milk Biscuits,

Broiled Fillet of Beef, Mushroom Sauce,

Peas,
Shaddock Sherbet,
Quail on Toast, Brown Sauce,
Baked Macaroni,
Lettuce Salad, French Dressing,

Wafers, Neufchâtel,
Coffee Jelly, Whipped Cream,
Fruit, Bonbons,

Coffee.

AN OYSTER SUPPER.

Raw Oysters on the Half Shell,
Oyster Soup,
Fried Oysters Garnished with Cress and Slices of Lemon,
Cold Slaw,
Chicken Salad, Water Crackers,
Oyster Croquettes, Sauce Hollandaise,
Peas,
Lettuce Salad, French Dressing,
Toasted Cheese,
Coffee.

A SIMPLE CHRISTMAS DINNER.

Cream of Celery Soup,
Creamed Fish, Potato Puff,
Roasted Turkey, Bread Stuffing,
Cranberry Sauce,
Mashed Potatoes, Canned Peas,
Stewed Turnips,
Lettuce Salad, French Dressing,
Water Crackers, Cheese,
Plain Plum Pudding, Hard Sauce,
Coffee.

VEGETARIAN MENUS.
SPRING.

BREAKFAST.
Shaddocks,
Wheat Granules, Sugar and Cream,
Stewed Potatoes, Omelet,
Gems, Coffee.

LUNCH.
Cream of Potato Soup,
Rice Croquettes, Tomato Sauce,
Lettuce with French Dressing,
Wafers, Cheese,
Baked Apples.

DINNER.

Mock Bisque Soup,

Salted Almonds, — Celery,
Cabbage, — Cream Sauce,

Sweet Potato Croquettes,
Salad of String Beans, French Dressing,

Wafers, — Cheese,
Batter Pudding with Canned Blackberries, — Hard Sauce,

Coffee.

SUMMER.

BREAKFAST.

Strawberries,
Molded Farina, Sugar and Cream,

Broiled Tomatoes, — Cream Sauce,
Muffins, — Coffee.

LUNCH.

Fried Egg Plant, — Sliced Tomatoes,

Brown Bread and Butter,
Mayonnaise of Cauliflower,

Wafers, — Cheese,

Iced Tea.

DINNER.

Asparagus Soup,

Macaroni Croquettes, — Tomato Sauce,

Stuffed Potatoes,
Macédoine Salad,

Wafers, — Cheese,

Frozen Strawberries,
Coffee.

SUPPER

Corn Fritters, — Brown Bread,
Sliced Tomatoes,
Fruit, — Wafers.

AUTUMN.

Breakfast.

Melons,
Oatmeal, Sugar and Cream,

Fried Squash,   Tomato Catsup,

Water-cress,

Gluten Gems,   Coffee.

Lunch.

Stuffed Egg-Plant,   Raw Tomatoes,

Salad of Lettuce, Peppers,
Fruit.

Dinner.

Cream of Corn Soup,

Stuffed Baked Tomatoes,   Lima Beans,

Boiled Rice,
Cauliflower with Cream Sauce,

String Beans,   French Dressing,

Wafers, Cheese,
Peach Pudding, Hard Sauce,
Coffee.

Supper.

Scalloped Potatoes,   Milk Biscuit,

Salad of Cucumbers and Tomatoes,
Compote of Pears, Wafers,
Tea.

WINTER.

Breakfast.

Baked Apples,   Grits, Sugar and Cream,

Omelet,   Baked Potatoes,

Muffins, Coffee.

Lunch.

Macaroni Croquettes,   Tomato Sauce,

Endive Salad,

Gingerbread,   Cocoa.

Dinner.

Salsify Soup,

Boiled Cabbage,   Caper Sauce,

Parsnip Fritters,   Stuffed Potatoes,

Stewed Canned Tomatoes,

Mayonnaise of Celery,

Wafers,   Cheese,

Apple Pie,

Coffee.

A SIMPLE THANKSGIVING DINNER.

Tomato Soup,

Boiled Haddock,   Drawn Butter,

French Fried Potatoes,

Roasted Chicken, Giblet Sauce,

Cranberries,

Boiled Rice,   Peas,

Mayonnaise of Celery,

Wafers,   Cheese,

Mince Pie,   Pumpkin Custard,

Coffee.

A GENTLEMEN'S FISH SUPPER.

Raw Oysters in a Block of Ice,

Fried Black Bass,   Parsley Sauce,

Stewed Potatoes,

Lobster Cutlets,   Cream Sauce,

Tea Biscuits,

Mayonnaise of Salmon,

Welsh Rarebit,

Coffee.

CHRISTMAS DINNER.

Cherrystone Oysters on Half Shell,
                          Clear Soup with Croûtons,
     Fried Smelts, Sauce Piquant,
                          French Fried Potatoes,
        Roasted Wild Turkey, Oyster Sauce,
                  Cranberry Sauce,
Boiled Rice,   Cauliflower,
                       Peas,
                  Orange Sherbet,
        Roasted Goose, Apple Sauce,
           Sweet Potato Croquettes,
             Mayonnaise of Celery,
  Water Biscuits,   Edam,
              Plum Pudding, Hard Sauce,
Nuts,   Fruits,   Raisins,
                       Coffee.

AN EMERGENCY DINNER OF CANNED GOODS.

              Cream of Tomato Soup,
  Boiled Salt of Mackerel, Parsley Sauce,
                                Lyonnaise Potatoes,
         Timbale of Macaroni, Cream Sauce,
      String Beans.
                       French Omelet with Peas,
         Lettuce Salad, French Dressing
Wafers,   Cheese,
                  Canned Fruit,
                  Coffee.

INDEX.

AMERICAN salad dressing, 124
Anchovy salad, 130
Apple jelly, 146, 147
Apples, to can, 140
  spiced, 152
Artichoke soup, 109
Artichokes, baked, 13
  French, 12
  fried, 13
  à l'Italienne, 14
  as a basis for jardinière, 13
  stuffed, 14
  Jerusalem, 14
    (à la lyonnaise), 15
    pickled, 16
    (à la vinaigrette), 13
Asparagus, 142
  in ambush, 17
  boiled, 16
  canned, 142
  escalloped, 18
  à la Hollandaise, 18
  peas, 19
  salad, 130
  stewed, 17
  soup, 110
Autumn bills of fare, 163, 164, 165

BAKED beans, 20
  Balls, chicken forcemeat, 109
  pop-corn, 156
Barley soup, 111
Bean croquettes, 22
  polenta, 22
Beans, 143
  baked, 20
  butter, 24
  case-knife, 24
  French, 24
  kidney, with brown sauce, 21
    à la maitre d'hotel, 20
  Lima, 23
    à la poulette, 23
    dried, 23
    and corn, 46
  red, 22
  string, 19
    with cream, 19
  white, sautés, 21
Beet salad, 131
Beets, boiled, 24

Beets with cream sauce, 24
  pickled, 25
  silver, 25
Bills of fare, 157
  for autumn, 163, 164, 165
  for spring, 158, 159, 160
  for summer, 161, 162, 163
  for winter, 165
Bisque of turnip, 120
Black bean soup, 118
Blackberry jelly, 148
Blackberries, to can, 140
Borecole, 26
Boulettes of potato, 80
Brandied peaches, 149
Bread, sweet potato, 89
Breakfasts, wedding, 168
Broccoli, 25
Broiled mushrooms, 60
  tomatoes, 101
Browned sweet potatoes, 89
  turnips, 103
Brussels sprouts, 25
  sprouts sautés, 26
Butter beans, 24
  tomato, 103

CABBAGE, boiled, 27
  Charleston, 29
  fried, 30
  lettuce, with gravy, 59
  pickled, 31
  salad, 132
  scalloped, 29
  stewed, 28
  stuffed, 28
  with corned beef, 27
  with Parmesan, 29
  red, à la flamande, 30
    pickled, 31
  German style, 30
Cakes, corn, griddle, 42
Canned fruits, 140
  apples, 140
  blackberries, 140
  cherries, 141
  peaches, 141
  pears, 141
  plums, 141
  quinces, 142
  quince and apple, 140

INDEX

Canned vegetables, 138
  asparagus, 142
  Lima beans, 143
  string beans, 143
  citron, 144
  corn, 143
    and tomatoes, 144
  gumbo and tomatoes, 144
  mushrooms, to stew, 61
  peas, 144
  tomatoes, 144
  peas, how to cook, 73
Canning, 138
Capsicums, to pickle, 75
Cardinal salad, 134
Carrot marmalade, 34
Carrots, pickled, 33
  stewed, 33, 34
Case-knife beans, 24
Casserole, potato, 87
Catsup, cucumber, 53
  tomato No. 1, 105
    No. 2, 105
  cold tomato, 106
  English tomato, 106
Cauliflower, baked, 36
  with cream sauce, 34
  au gratin, 36
  pickled, 36
  stewed, 35
  salad, 131
Celeriac, 38
Celery, à la Française, 37
  fried, 37
  au jus, 39
  stewed, 38
  with tomato sauce, 37
  in stuffed tomatoes, 102
  salad, 132
  soup, 112
  vinegar, 152
  turnip-rooted, 38
Chard, Swiss, 25
Cherries, to can, 141
  spiced, 152
Chicory with cream, 39
Chicken forcemeat balls, 109
  salad, 128
Chili vinegar, 152
Chips, Saratoga, 84
Chowder, corn, 48
  potato, 86
Christmas dinner, 175
  dinner, a simple, 171
Citron, 144
Cock-a-leekie, 121
Cold slaw, 32
Combinations of foods, 10
Corn, 143
  boiled on cob, 39
  boiled in husk, 40
  chowder, 48
  cold, 42
  fricasseed with okra, 65
  fritters, 40
  oysters, 46

Corn, pickled, small ears, 44
  pudding, 47
    southern, 46
  salted, 45
  scalloped, 41
  soup, 112
  stewed, 42
    with Lima beans, 46
    with tomatoes, 41
  in tins, 45
  warmed over, 42
  and tomatoes, 144
  gems, 42
  griddle cakes, 42
  how to dry, 43
  dry—how to cook, 45
  to hull, 43
  to pop, 156
Corn-salad, 44, 135
Corned beef, with cabbage, 27
Crab apple jelly, 148
Crab salad, 129
Cream salad dressing, 125
  vegetable soups, 109
Croquettes, bean, 22
  potato, 79
  sweet potato, 89
Croûtons, 111
Cucumber catsup, 53
  mangoes, 54
  pickles, oiled, 52
  salad, 132
Cucumbers, with cream sauce, 49
  fried, 50
  in butter, 50
  pickled, 52
  salted for pickling, 50, 51
  stewed, 48
  stuffed, 49
  sweet, pickled, 53
Currant jelly, 149
Curried tomatoes, 101
Custard, white potato, 87

DAMSON jelly, 149
  Dandelion salad, 135
Dandelions, German style, 55
  wilted, 54
Delmonico potatoes, 82
Dinner, Christmas, 175
  a simple Christmas, 171
    Thanksgiving, 174
  an emergency, of canned goods, 175
Dock, narrow, 55
  sour, 55
Dredged tomatoes, 100
Dressing, French, 124
  American salad, 124
  cream salad, 125
  mayonnaise, 127
  Mrs. Rorer's salad, 126
  potato salad, 126
  salad, without oil, 125
Dried bean soup, 117
  corn, to cook, 44

INDEX. 179

Dried mushrooms, 62
Dry pumpkins for pies, 90
Dutch lettuce, 60

EGG-PLANT, baked, 56
   in batter, 56
   dressed, 56
   farcied, 57
   fried, 55
Egg salad, 133
Egyptian salad, 137
Emergency dinner, of canned goods, 175
Endive, 55
   salad, 135
English pea porridge, 116
   tomato catsup, 106

FARE, bills of, 157
   Figs, tomato, 102
Fish supper, a gentlemen's, 174
Flavored vinegars, 152
Foods, combinations of, 10
Forcemeat balls, chicken, 109
French artichoke salad, 131
   artichokes, 12
   beans, 24
   dressing, 124
Fritters, corn, 40
   parsnip, 70
   salsify, 96
Fruit jellies, 146
Fruits, to can, 140
   to serve, 154, 155

GEMS, corn, 42
   German salad, 133
Glazed onions, 68
Grape jelly, 149
Green tomato pickles, 107
Griddle cakes, corn, 42
Gumbo, 63
   and tomatoes, 144

HERBS, to dry, 154
   Honey, tomato, 107
Horse-radish vinegar, 152
Hotch-potch, 121

ICED tomatoes, 102
   Italian salad, 133

JAM, rhubarb, 145
   Jelly, apple, 146, 147
      crab apple, 148
      blackberry, 148
      currant, 149
      damson, 149
      grape, 149
      peach, 149
      rhubarb, 149

Jellies, fruit, 146
Jerusalem, artichokes, 14
   à la lyonnaise, 15
   pickled, 16
   à la vinaigrette, 15
Julienne soup, 119

KALE, 26
   with pork, 27
Kale turnip, 32
Kidney beans, with brown sauce, 21
   à la maitre d'hotel, 20
Kohl-rabi, 32

LEEKS, 57
   stewed, 57
Lentil rolls, 58
   soup, 119
Lentils, 57
   with rice, 58
Lettuce, 59
   cabbage, with gravy, 59
   Dutch, 60
   salad, 135
Lima bean soup, 111
   beans, 23, 143
   à la poulette, 23
   and corn, 46
   dried, 23
   to pickle, 150
Lobster salad, 130
Lunch, 169, 170

MANGOES, cucumber, 54
   pepper, 73
   tomato, 104
Marmalade, carrot, 34
   yellow tomato, 104
Martynias, 63
Mayonnaise dressing, 127
   tomato salad, 136
Meat, salt, with pumpkin, 92
Menus, vegetarian, 171, 172, 173
   autumn, 173
   spring, 171
   summer, 172
   winter, 173
Mushrooms, 61
   baked, 60
   broiled, 60
   dried, 62
   stewed, No. 1, 62
      No. 2, 63
   canned, to stew, 61

NASTURTIUM blossom, 135

OKRA, 63
   boiled, 64
   stewed, 65

INDEX.

Okra, fricasseed with corn, 65
    with rice, 64
    with tomatoes, 64
Omelet with peas, 72
Onion salad, 137
    soubise, 68
    soup, 120
    vinegar, 69, 153
Onions baked, 66
    boiled, 65
    fried, 66
    glazed, 68
    pickled, 69
    scalloped, 67
    stewed, 67
    stuffed, 67
    Spanish, 66
Oyster plant, boiled, 96
    soup, 114
    supper, 171
Oysters, corn, 46

PARSNIP fritters, 70
    Parsnips, baked, 70
    boiled, with cream sauce, 69
    fried, 70
Parsley, pickled, 33
Pea soup, 112
    from canned peas, 113
Peas asparagus, 19
Peas, 144
    green, 71
    with cream sauce, 73
    with omelet, 72
    how to can, 72
Peach jelly, 149
Peaches, brandied, 149
    to can, 141
    spiced, 152
Pears, to can, 141
    spiced, 152
Pepper grass, 135
Pepper mangoes, 73
    sauce, 74
Peppers, pickled, 74
    stuffed, 75
Pickled artichokes, Jerusalem, 16
    beets, 25
    cabbage, 31
        red, 31
    carrots, 33
    parsley, 33
    peppers, 74
    onions, 69
    radish pods, 94
    tomatoes, 102
Pickles, cauliflower, 36
    corn, small ears, 44
    cucumbers, oiled, 52
        small, 52
        sweet, 53
        salted for, 50, 51
    green tomatoes, 107
Pie, white potato, 88

Pie, sweet potato, 90
    pumpkin, 91
    rhubarb, 94
Plums, to can, 141
    spiced, 152
Pods, sugar pea, 73
Poke stalks, 76
Polenta bean, 22
Pop-corn balls, 156
Pork, with kale, 27
Porridge, English pea, 116
Potato, boulettes of, 80
    casserole, 87
    chowder, 86
    croquettes, 79
    custard, white, 87
    pie, white, 88
    puff, 80
    salad, 136
        dressing, 126
    sautés 83
    soufflé, 86
    soup, 113
Potatoes, 76
    baked, 85
        with meat, 86
    boiled, 77
    Delmonico, 82
    à la duchesse, 84
    French, fried, 82
    hashed, browned, 81
        browned, in the oven, 82
        with cream 82
    à la Hollandaise, 84
    lyonnaise, 83
    à la maitre d'hôtel, 87
    mashed, 79
    panned, 82
    ragout of, 84
    scalloped, 78
    steamed, 78
    stewed, 80
    stuffed, 85
    with cream sauce, 81
    with turnips, 108
    sweet, 88
        baked, 88
        browned, 89
        croquettes, 89
        roasted, 88
        mashed, southern style, 89
Pot au feu, 122
Powder, soup, 153
Proper vegetables to serve with meats, 11, 12
Pudding, corn, 47
    southern corn, 46
Pumpkin, baked, 92
    chips, preserved, 146
    pie, 91
    preserved, 90
        in pieces, 91
    with salt meat, 92
Pumpkins, dried for pies, 90
Purée of sorrel, 97
    of vegetable soup, 115

INDEX. 181

Q UINCES, to can, 142
  spiced, 152

R ADISH PODS, pickled, 94
  Radishes, 93
    winter, with cream sauce, 93
Ragout of potatoes, 84
Rhubarb jam, 145
  jelly, 149
  pie, 94
  stewed, 94
  vinegar, 95
  wine, 95
Rice with lentils, 58
  with okra, 64
  soup, 114
  as a vegetable, 95
Rolls, lentils, 58
Ruta baga, 109

S ALAD, anchovy, 130
  artichoke, French, 131
  asparagus, 130
  beet, 131
  cabbage, 132
  cardinal, 134
  cauliflower, 131
  celery, 132
  chicken, 128
  crab, 129
  cucumber, 132
  of cucumber and tomato, 132
  dandelion, 135
  egg, 133
  Egyptian, 137
  endive, 135
  German, 133
  Italian, 133
  lettuce, 135
  lobster, 130
  Macédoine, 135
  onion, 137
  sour orange, 147
  potato, 136
  salmon, 130
  sardine, 130
  shad roe, 130
  shrimp, 130
  of string beans, 131
  sorrel, 135
  summer, 135
  Swedish, 134
  sweet-bread, 129
  tomato and celery, 137
  veal, 129
Salad dressing, American, 124
  cream, 125
  French, 124
  mayonnaise, 127
  without oil, 125
  potato, 126
  Mrs. Rorer's, 126
Salads, 122
  their preparation, 123

Salsify, boiled, 96
  fried, 96
  fritters, 96
Sauce, pepper, 74
  soubise, 68
Sauerkraut, 32
Season for pickling, 150, 151
Silver beet, 25
Sorrel, purée of, 97
Soubise onion, 68
Soufflé potato, 86
Sour dock, 55
Southern corn pudding, 46
Soup, artichoke, 109
  asparagus, 110
  barley, 111
  black bean, 118
  dried bean, 117
  Lima bean, 111
  mock bisque, 115
  celery, 112
  corn, 112
  Crécy, 116
  Julienne, 119
  lentil, 119
  à la mousquetaire, 122
  onion, 120
  oyster plant, 114
  of Palestine, 110
  pea, 112
    from canned peas, 113
  potato, 113
  rice, 114
  salsify, 114
  clear vegetable, 118
  purée of vegetable, 115
  vegetable without meat, 117
Soup powder, 153
Soups, cream vegetables, 109
Spanish onions, 66
Spiced apples, 152
  cantaloupe, 151
  cherries, 152
  peaches, 152
  peas, 152
  plums, 152
  quinces, 152
  water-melon, 152
Spinach, 96
  with cream, 97
  for garnishing, 97
Sprouts, Brussels, 25
  boiled, plain, 26
  sautés, 26
Sprouts, turnip, 109
Squash, fried, 98
  summer, 98
  with melted butter, 98
Stalks, poke, 76
String beans, 19
  with cream, 19
  to pickle, 150
Stuffed peppers, 75
Succotash, 47
Sugar pea pods, 73
Supper, a gentlemen's fish, 174

Sweet potato bread, 89
    croquettes, 89
    pie, 90
Sweet potatoes, 88
    baked, 88
    browned, 89
    mashed, Southern style, 89
    roasted, 88
Swiss chard, 25

THANKSGIVING dinner, a simple, 174
Tomato butter, 103
    catsup No. 1, 105
    No. 2, 105
    cold, 106
    English, 106
    farci, 100
    figs, 102
    honey, 107
    mangoes, 104
    marmalade, yellow, 104
    pickles, green, 107
    preserves, ripe, 103
Tomato and celery salad, 137
Tomatoes, 144
    baked, 99
    broiled, 101
    curried, 101
    dredged, 100
    fried, 100
    iced, 102
    pickled, 102
    preserved, green, 104
    on half shell, 101
    stewed, 98
    stuffed, 99
        with celery, 102
    and corn, 144

Tomatoes and gumbo, 144
    with okra, 64
    with stewed corn, 41
Turnip, kale, 32
    sprouts, 109
    tops, 109, 135
Turnips, bisque of, 120
    browned, 108
    mashed, 108
    with potatoes, 108
    with cream sauce, 108

VEAL salad, 129
    Vegetable soup, clear, 118
    soups, with meat, 117
        without meat, 117
Vegetables, how to cook, 9
    how to serve, 11
    canned, 139
Vinegar, celery, 152
    Chili, 152
    horse-radish, 152
    onion, 69, 153
    rhubarb, 95
    Tarragon, 153

WATER-CRESS, 135
    Water-melon rind, 145
        spiced, 152
Wedding breakfasts, 168
Wilted dandelions, 54
Wine, rhubarb, 95
Winter bills of fare, 165
    radishes with cream sauce, 93

YELLOW tomato marmalade, 104

www.ingramcontent.com/pod-product-compliance
Lightning Source LLC
Chambersburg PA
CBHW032154160426
43197CB00008B/914